D WALK

OUGH OF SOUTHWARK

CUNARDIA

Conceived, designed and produced by

The Open Agency
Mill House
8 Mill Street
London SE1 2BA
www.openthebook.com
+44 (0)20 7740 7000

Written by **Elspeth Wills**

First published 2005
© The Open Agency Limited

All images © Cunard Line or The Open Agency

ISBN 0-9542451-5-6

Printed in China.

CUNARDIA

A steamer trunk of titbits, trivia and trifles.

TAKE A STROLL DOWN CUNARD STREET

The Cunard shipping line has made its mark on the globe in surprising ways. Take a street map of London, Los Angeles or New York and there is a Cunard Crescent or Cunard Close. Towns and cities in several continents celebrate some of Cunard's greatest liners.

Cunard has entered the English language. Older passengers may still remember suffering from Cunard thumb when they tried to open their porthole. In Liverpool and Southampton, seafarers still walk with Cunard feet, the rolling gait resulting from years of keeping their balance on storm lashed decks. Some stewards still call themselves Cunard Yanks, recalling the era of the early 1950s when they brought back fridges, nylons and the sounds of New York soul and jazz to war-torn Britain.

Since 1840 when Samuel Cunard founded the British and North American Royal Mail Steam Packet Company to carry Her Majesty's mails across the Atlantic, Cunarders have gone down in history – the Carpathia's rescue of the survivors from the Titanic; the tragic sinking of the Lusitania; the building of the Queen Mary at the height of the world Depression; and the ferrying of GIs across the Atlantic during the Second World War. As well as millions of emigrants, holidaymakers and businessmen Cunard passenger lists have included the names of world leaders, millionaires and the glitterati of the entertainment world. Sir Winston Churchill and Cary Grant, Walt Disney and the Windsors all shared the experience of crossing on the Queens.

On going up the gangway, passengers entered a different world with its own customs, fashions and daily routine. They read their Ocean Times over breakfast and strolled a mile along the prom deck: they learned how to play shuffleboard and tennequoits and bet on the pool. In the Twenties the smart set went slumming in third class while a decade later every 'It-girl' posed with a lifebelt against the backdrop of a deck rail. By the end of a crossing, some passengers could tell 'fore' from 'aft' and 'bow' from 'stern' while others still regularly lost themselves in the maze of corridors and stairwells between their cabin and the dining room. All had their stories to tell of their Atlantic crossing, whether surviving the worst storm that the captain had ever encountered or a fleeting romance on a moonlit deck.

Above Passenger mementoes of 20th century crossings.

Above Cunard staff featured in the Cunard Magazine, 1923.

The crew's world was different again, a completely separate system of alleys and storerooms centred on the High Street, the passageway that ran the length of the ship. They had to know who was who from the master-at-arms to the black squad and how they fitted into the complex hierarchy headed by the captain. Crew who dealt with passengers had to learn the niceties of etiquette – where to place the cutlery for a five course gala dinner; how to address an archbishop or when 'to be seen but not heard'. Being caught smoking on deck or asleep in a passenger cabin could result in a fine or instant dismissal.

Over the years Cunard has become a legend, associated with glamour, safety and speed. For many passengers it was 'the only way to cross'. Few other than the seasick disagreed with Cunard's 1950s claim that 'Getting there is half the fun.' 'You will find in your Cunarder not just a method of transportation but a way of life. … She is anything you want her to be.' The Cunard brand was recognised throughout the world from the tops of the red and black funnels appearing over the horizon to the lion rampant that flew on the house flag.

Cunarders on film and in verse, summed up in statistics or immortalised by history – dip into this compendium of Cunardia and catch a glimpse of the world of Cunard over the last 165 years.

Above Pencil sketch for Cunard Magazine, 1923.

THE CUNARD LION
Symbol of an Empire

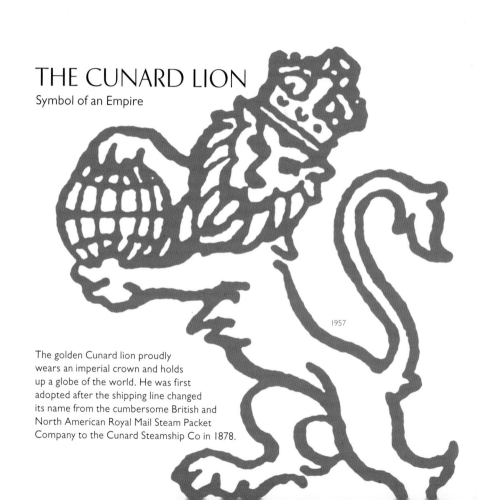

1957

The golden Cunard lion proudly
wears an imperial crown and holds
up a globe of the world. He was first
adopted after the shipping line changed
its name from the cumbersome British and
North American Royal Mail Steam Packet
Company to the Cunard Steamship Co in 1878.

1890

1930

1951

1953

1969

2005

CUNARD ON FILM

Cunarders have played a starring role as film sets

The Aquitania featured in a number of silent movies. After Cunard made a promotional film on the liner in the 1920s, a copy was put aside to be shown in a hundred years time.

John Francis Dillon filmed part of his silent comedy 'Too Much Money' (1926) on board the Franconia II.

Director William Wyler's 'Dodsworth' (1936) about infidelity at sea was partly set on the Queen Mary.

'She Shall Have Music' (1936), a vehicle for the bandleader Jack Hylton, tapped into the craze for all things maritime in the year of the Queen Mary's maiden voyage.

'The Lady Eve' (1941), where Barbara Stanwyck has Henry Fonda bewitched and bemused on an ocean voyage, used the Mauretania II as stand-in for the SS Southern Queen.

In 'Gentlemen Prefer Blondes' (1953) Marilyn Monroe and Jane Russell played two man-hunting show girls prowling around an ocean liner. Some of the sets were used previously in 'Titanic' (1953) but were refurbished to resemble the Queen Mary.

The Queen Mary was the first liner to feature on Cinerama. 'Cinerama Holiday' (1954) showed her sailing into New York at the end of a crossing. Crowds queued outside cinemas on both sides of the Atlantic to marvel at the new wide-screen technology.

In 1957 Tommy Steele starred in 'Rock Around the World' a biopic about his early life. In one scene he fell out with the chief steward, mirroring his real life experience as a Cunard waiter.

Peter Sellers, Ringo Starr and George Harrison filmed scenes for 'The Magic Christian' (1969) on board the QE2.

Since finding her final berth as a museum, the Queen Mary has featured in several films including 'Assault on a Queen' (1966), 'The Poseidon Adventure' (1972), 'SOS Titanic' (1979) and 'Britannic' (1997).

Above Filming 'Too Much Money' on board Franconia II.

Kenneth More and Roland Calver sailed on the Queen Elizabeth while filming 'Next to No Time' (1959), a comedy set on the ship.

Cunarders have also made regular television appearances. Scenes from the classic 'Brideshead Revisited' (1981) were shot on the QE2 masquerading as the Queen Mary. Passengers on the voyage had the added excitement of appearing as extras.

In 1995 a special episode of Britain's favourite soap 'Coronation Street' was filmed on the QE2.

Even Cunard's offices have appeared on screen, especially those set in Liverpool. When the Detective Chief Superintendent played by Laurence Olivier interviewed a passenger clerk about the movements of a passenger to New York in 'Bunny Lake is Missing' (1965), the set was Cunard's Lower Regent St office in London.

FIRST 6 & 8 SHELLS
MANUFACTURED IN GREAT BRITAIN
BY LADY OPERATORS
AT
CUNARD S.S.C⁰ˢ SHELL WORKS

RIMROSE R⁰   1915.

SUPPORTING THE WAR EFFORT
Cunard's land based activities 1914-18

Cunard played a major role on land as well as on the ocean during the First World War.

In addition to managing 400 ships on behalf of the Government and releasing its own staff to serve in the Forces, Cunard built and ran what was then England's largest aircraft factory at Aintree. At its engine works cruisers, transports, seaplane carriers and other vessels were fitted out and gun beds, artillery wheels, parts for submarines and mines were manufactured. Even the Cunard laundry was taken over to serve military hospitals.

Above Commemorative booklet of Cunard's clerical staff who served in the Forces during the First World War.

Cunard's engine plant on Merseyside was converted into a munitions factory employing 1000 workers, to turn out hundreds of thousands of shells. Women working on shell filling lines risked poisoning and explosions from handling TNT. They were known as canaries as the chemicals turned their skin yellow. There were good times too. The works had its in-house concert party, 'The High Explosives', who regularly entertained the workers.

Even the new headquarters building on Liverpool's Pier Head did not escape the imprint of war. Carved shields on the frieze facing the river represented the arms of the Allies including Japan, Serbia and Montenegro. Inside the building staff worked overtime to service the liners as they carried troops across the Atlantic, and in their spare time raised thousands of pounds for the war effort. Even Cunard's ferry tender, Skirmisher, was called up to provide trips down the Mersey for wounded troops.

After the Armistice was declared on 11th November, 1918, the Cunard headquarters was decked with banners and flags to welcome back demobbed employees. On hearing that the War was over, the general manager of Cunard's London office called staff together and announced that this was probably the greatest day in the history of the world. The staff sang 'Rule Britannia' and 'God Save the King', recited the Ten Commandments and then danced to ragtime.

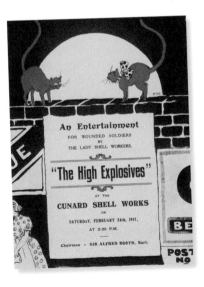

CUNARD STREET
Cunard addresses around the world

Cities, towns and ports have honoured Samuel Cunard and his famous shipping line by naming streets and avenues, parks and schools after him.

Cunard Avenue East Baton Rouge, Louisiana	*Cunard Place* Mount Pearl, Newfoundland
Cunard Avenue Cheektowaga, New York State	*Cunard Road* Bootle, England
Cunard Avenue Southampton, England	*Cunard Road* Fayette County, West Virginia
Cunard Avenue New Castle County, Delaware	*Cunard Road* Park Royal, London
Cunard Avenue New Brighton, England	*Cunard Road* Huber Heights, Ohio
Cunard Avenue Deptford, New Jersey	*Cunard Road* Liverpool, England
Cunard Close Durban, South Africa	*Cunard Road* North Acton, London
Cunard Close Winchmore Hill, London	*Cunard Street* Laval, Quebec
Cunard Close Manchester, England	*Cunard Street* Halifax, Nova Scotia
Cunard Close Wallasey, England	*Cunard Street* Los Angeles, California
Cunard Court Clydebank, Scotland	*Cunard Street* Miramichi, New Brunswick
Cunard Crescent Enfield, London	*Cunard Street* Cardington, Ohio
Cunard Crescent Conception Bay, Newfoundland	*Cunard Street* Scarborough, Ontario
Cunard Crescent Mount Pearl, Newfoundland	*Cunard Street* Waldport, Oregon
Cunard Lane Johnstown, Pennsylvania	*Cunard Street* Boston, Massachusetts
Cunard Park Virginia Highlands, Atlanta	*Cunard Street* Pretoria, South Africa
Cunard Place Staten Island, New York	*Cunard Street* St John's, Newfoundland
Cunard Place East Baton Rouge, Louisiana	*Cunard Street* San Diego, California
Cunard Place London	*Cunard Street* Auckland, New Zealand
Cunard Place Winnipeg, Manitoba	*Cunard Street* Clydebank, Scotland

Opposite Cunard Street and Court, Clydebank where John Brown's shipyard built the Queens.
Below left to right Cunard Road, Liverpool; Cunard Walk, London; Cunard Place, London EC3; Cunard Avenue, Southampton.

FINAL FATE

The end of Cunarders' careers

When a vessel came to the end of its service with Cunard, its fate was by no means always the scrap yard. Many ships continued their adventures under other flags.

Cunard's first ship, the Britannia, came to an ignominious end. Retired in 1848 she served until 1880 in the Prussian navy. She finally sank after being used for target practice.

Like several other early Cunarders the America was converted to sail after she retired from the fleet in 1866, being renamed the Coalgacondor.

The Scotia, Cunard's last paddle steamer and the finest ship of her day, enjoyed a lengthy second career as a telegraph cable laying vessel, after being sold in 1874.

After 119 crossings for Cunard, the Parthia was sold in 1883. She finally retired after 86 years at sea, nine changes of ownership, two changes of name and service as an emigrant ship, trooper, gold rush carrier, blockade runner, Arctic cruise liner, wartime supply ship, cargo vessel and log carrying barge.

A devastating fire broke out while the Lucania was laid up in Liverpool in 1909. After firemen spent several hours trying unsuccessfully to put out the blaze, she was towed into the middle of the harbour coming to rest on the mud. Although crippled beyond repair, she still managed to sail under her own steam to the breaker's yard.

After two onboard fires attributed to faulty wiring, the Berengaria was withdrawn from service in 1938. Two hundred men were employed to dismantle her. With the outbreak of war, their services were required on more urgent duties and it was not until 1946 that the old lady's hull was finally broken up.

In 1949, while berthed in Southampton, one of the Aquitania's decks split in a rainstorm causing water to cascade below on to the heads of some Board of Trade surveyors. They were enjoying lunch after granting her a certificate of seaworthiness. She was scrapped shortly thereafter.

After the Queen Mary crossed for the last time in 1967, she was put up for auction. The highest bidder was the City of Long Beach, California who offered $3.4m dollars to turn her into a visitor attraction. Many of her fittings were sold. One interior decorator bought an assortment of odds and ends for $20,000 and made $1m selling them as souvenirs, including crested chamber pots for use as champagne buckets. Among his customers were Lucille Ball, Frank Sinatra and Dean Martin.

The Queen Elizabeth was put up for sale in 1968. Her new owner who planned to convert her into a convention centre in Port Everglades went bankrupt. Shipowner C. Y. Tung then bought her to turn her into a floating university, but she caught fire and sank in Hong Kong Harbour.

The Green Goddess Caronia II turned pale in 1967 when sold, renamed the Caribia and painted white. After two disastrous cruises, she was laid up for six years while the lawyers wrangled over her fate. She even incurred a 'parking ticket' for docking in the Hudson without a permit. Bought by a Taiwanese shipbreaking firm, she suffered the indignity of being towed across the Pacific until Tropical Storm Mary finally grounded her on the rocks outside Guam Harbour.

After serving on the Canadian run for nearly a decade, the Ivernia II was refitted for cruising and renamed Franconia III. She was sold in 1973 to the Soviet Union as a cruise ship, named after the Russian opera star Feodor Shalyapin.

Below Crazy hat competition during the Queen Mary's final voyage to Long Beach.

A DRINK AT THE CUNARD

Cunard and Liverpool

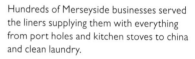

Cunard has had more connections with the city of Liverpool on the river Mersey than with anywhere else in the world.

Before their merger in 1934, both Cunard and White Star Lines had their headquarters in the city. After the merger many thousands of Liverpudlians continued to work for 'The C'nard'.

Although express liners like the Mauretania and the Queen Mary sailed from Southampton from 1919, they still carried the name 'Liverpool' on their stern as their port of registry.

Several Cunard liners were built on Merseyside including the Cephalonia (1882), the Samaria II (1922) and the Mauretania II (1939).

Hundreds of Merseyside businesses served the liners supplying them with everything from port holes and kitchen stoves to china and clean laundry.

At the beginning of the 20th century 90% of Cunard's seafarers came from Merseyside. Captains and senior officers lived in the grander suburbs, often within sight or sound of the sea. Many of the lower ranks spent their shore leave in one of the steep streets of brick terraced houses running off Scotland Road.

The names of local streets, the great palace of the Cunard Headquarters on the Pier Head, the liners in the docks, the pubs where crew drank on the night before sailing day - there was no escaping Cunard in Liverpool.

Above Liverpool's Cunard and White Star pubs.

CARD SHARPS & CON MEN
Not Wanted on Voyage

Professional gamblers and tricksters were a hazard of life at sea. On the Berengaria one of the junior pursers' duties was to patrol the smokeroom announcing: 'Ladies and Gentlemen. We have reason to believe there are card sharpers aboard.' Passengers then played at their own risk. The face of one card sharper who had made a fortune on the liners was so well known that he could no longer hoodwink passengers. They continued to play with him for the honour of being able to say that they had pitted their wits against him.

Card sharps saw the Cunarders as rich pickings right from the start. In 1842 Charles Dickens discreetly warned a fellow passenger on the Britannia of the presence of a 'card shark'.

One legendary tactic of early 20th century confidence tricksters was extortion. The target was usually a wealthy and flirtatious married man who was lured into a compromising situation by a female trickster. Playing the role of the 'outraged husband' her accomplice would burst into the cabin waving a revolver. The duped passenger paid up quietly to keep his wife in ignorance.

CHIN CHIN

The cocktail hour was the ultimate in liner chic and the Observation Bar the place to see and be seen

'In one's hand the martini trembles faintly. One feels the throb of the liner's thrust. Black ties and tuxedos, bare arms and pearls, a steady rise of conversation and laughter. Now is the moment of warmth and balance when every kind of communication seems easy - alone at sea on a common voyage, sharing the luxury of place and purpose. A tray of oranges stuck with beetroot roses offers hot canapés of bacon and liver.'

Author **Laurie Lee,** first class passenger on the Queen Mary.

Left Young film star Roger Moore on the Queen Mary.
Opposite, left Clark Gable enjoying a drink with the purser on the Queen Mary.
Opposite, right Comedian Peter Cook keeps fellow guests - including David Frost - entertained on the Queen Mary.

The actual mix of cocktails mirrored the fashion of the day.

1840 In the same year as Samuel Cunard's Britannia first set out on the high seas, James Pimms created the gin with a zing - Pimm's no 1.

1860 A Milanese cafe owner invented Campari.

1874 A barman at the Manhattan Club, New York created the Manhattan for Sir Winston Churchill's mother, a regular Cunard passenger, as was her son.

1915 A barman at Raffles Hotel invented the Singapore Sling tinted pink to appeal to women.

1921 Harry's Bar in Paris invented the Bloody Mary, originally called 'Buckets of Blood'.

1925 Through his novel 'The Great Gatsby' F. Scott Fitzgerald, himself a Cunard traveller, made the Mint Julep fashionable. By the 1950s liners were carrying up to 50lbs of mint leaves per crossing.

1933 President F. D. Roosevelt celebrated the end of Prohibition with a Martini.

1948 Guiseppe Cipriani of Harry's Bar in Venice created the Bellini called after the pink tones used by the famous Renaissance painter.

1955 The Queen Mary's head barman invented a cocktail in honour of the ship's Irish doctor Joseph Maguire. He called it JBM - Just Before Meals. It consisted of four fifths Irish whiskey, one fifth green chartreuse, a drop of honey and a squeeze of lemon juice.

1960 The Daiquiri became fashionable when President Kennedy declared it to be his favourite cocktail.

1975 The QE2's Queen's Grill bar served 43 different cocktails including the QE2 - a mixture of brandy, orange juice, grenadine, curacao and vermouth.

2000 Cocktails underwent a revival in the 1990s. Today the top liner favourites include Acapulco, Mudslide and Cosmopolitan.

THE CAPTAIN'S TABLE

On early Cunarders everyone ate at the captain's table

When author William Thackeray crossed on the Canada in 1852, 'Captain L came to dinner at eight bells as usual, talked a little to the persons right and left of him, and helped the soup with his accustomed politeness. Then he went on deck, and was back in a minute, and operated on the fish.'

By 1900 an invitation to the captain's table was an honour much sought after by the socially aspiring. Captain William Turner was more seaman than host. He described first class passengers as 'a load of bloody monkeys who are constantly chattering' and excused himself from the captain's table at the merest hint of fog. Passengers, however, loved the challenge of his gruff and aloof manner, some individuals choosing to travel only if he was in command. Baffled, Cunard transferred him to larger and larger liners: his fans always followed.

Sir James Charles, captain of the Mauretania in the 1920s, was the first to establish strict rules of etiquette at the captain's table.

Having been knighted for his war service, he demanded that guests wear full military decorations, putting many Americans at a disadvantage. Sir James was also a great trencherman. Whole roast oxen or small herds of gazelles, surmounted by hillocks of foie gras decorated with peacock feathers, were wheeled to his table where champagne was served in jeroboams and souffles were the size of chefs' hats. Confectioners spent hours creating centre pieces in carved ice or spun sugar: on one occasion an electrically illuminated Battle of Waterloo was carried in to the ship's orchestra playing Elgar.

Table 199 was the captain's table on the Queen Mary. Each day the list of 200 possible guests was whittled down to six or eight names. For three years after the Second World War, Captain Grattidge's only reading was 'Who's Who' and 'Who's Who in America'. One crew member recalled: 'A place on the captain's table was the ultimate goal for social climbing passengers and also for businessmen who could afford to buy the liner out of their own funds. Extravagance was the name of the game.'

When the Queen Mother joined Commodore Sir Ivan Thompson at the captain's table of the Queen Mary on a 1954 crossing there was not an empty seat in the dining room. Even those who usually liked to be fashionably late scrambled for a place.

Captain Thelwell of the Queen Mary kept a list of guests whom he had entertained, with comments for future reference. His entry for 10th August, 1955 read: 'Mrs C. Chaplin. A wash out. Never at the table.'

One elderly passenger on the QE2 was invited to dine at the captain's table after a relative wrote to Cunard telling them how much he was looking forward to the trip of a lifetime. When the captain arrived, the old man left, complaining 'I didn't save up all my life to dine with the crew!'

Left Cunard's Chairman hosted onboard parties when the liners were in dock, Scythia, 1890.
Below Commodore Bisset hosting the captain's t able on the Queen Elizabeth, 1947.

Bothnia

Caledonia
Scotia

Ultonia

Hibernia
Ivernia

Britannia

Cambria

Batavia

Saxonia

Alsatia

Franconia

Scythia

Gallia

Jura

Carinthia

Carpathia

Aquitania

Alps

Transylvania

Tuscania
Umbria
Etruria

Slavonia

Albania

Servia

Catalonia

Saragossa

Campania
Lucania

Olympus

Lusitania

Calabria

Cephalonia

Marathon

Tarifa

Etna

Laconia

Asia

Malta

Mauretania

Atlas

Tripoli

Algeria

IMPERIUM CUNARDIUM
Ship names and places

The Cunard Empire was global. When Samuel Cunard christened his first ship, Britannia, in 1840, he laid down two traditions which the names of the fleet followed for over a century. Most Cunarders were called after land masses - mountains, continents and Empires. Names were usually Latin in origin ending in 'ia'.

Abyssinia *(1870-1880)* the former name of Ethiopia which the Arabs once knew as 'habasah'

Acadia *(1840-1848)* the early name for part of Nova Scotia, Samuel Cunard's native land

Africa *(1850-1868)* possibly from the Latin word for 'sunny', Roman Africa was confined to the Mediterranean coast

Alaunia *(1913-1916)* called after the Alan tribe who with the Goths may have given their name to Catalonia in Spain

Albania *(1911-1912)* named in ancient times after the Albanoi tribe who lived in Illyria

Aleppo *(1865-1909)* the Syrian city which claims to be one of the oldest in the world

Taurus

Parthia

Aleppo

Palmyra

Lebanon

Sidon   Damascus

Palestine

Samaria

Persia

Media

Algeria *(1870-1882)* named after the Arabic word for 'island'

Alps *(1853-1859)* Europe's highest mountain range

America *(1848-1868)* named in honour of the Italian explorer Amerigo Vespucci who discovered the mainland of the New World

Andania *(1913-1918)* an ancient city in South West Greece famous for worshipping the earth goddess Demeter

Andes *(1852-1859)* the highest mountain range in South America

Aquitania *(1914-1949)* the Roman province corresponding to modern south west France

Arabia *(1853-1864)* the ancient kingdom that grew wealthy on its trade in frankincense and myrrh

Ascania *(1911-1918)* named after the Askaeni, the tribe from Asia Minor who first settled in Scandinavia

Asia *(1850-1867)* the ancient Greek for the word 'East'

Athenia *(1923-1935)* celebrating the capital of Greek civilization

Atlas *(1860-1896)* the North African mountain range called after the giant whom Zeus punished by making him carry heaven and earth on his shoulders

Ausonia *(1911-1918)* an ancient name for Italy, from Auson, one of Ulysses' sons

Australasian *(1860-1876)* the continent which the Cunarder's name personalised

Balbec *(1853-1884)* ancient Syrian city which the Greeks renamed Heliopolis 'city of the sun'

Batavia *(1870-1877)* the Latin name for the Netherlands once inhabited by the Germanic tribe Batavi

Bothnia *(1874-1896)* an arm of the Baltic sea between Sweden and Finland

Britannia *(1840-1848)* named after Samuel Cunard's adopted land

Caledonia *(1840-1850)* the Roman name for Scotland, the most northerly outpost of their Empire

California *(1907-1917)* one of two Cunarders called after an American State

Cambria *(1844-1860)* the Roman name for Wales

Campania *(1893-1918)* the Roman province whose present-day capital is Naples

Carmania *(1905-1931)* a region of ancient Persia

Caronia *(1905-1933)* a town in Sicily which took its name from the Greek 'new house'

Carpathia *(1903-1918)* derived from the Albanian word 'carpe' rock giving rise to the name of the tribe and the mountain range

R.M.S. Ascania

Canada *(1848-1867)* the world's biggest village named after the Huron-Iroquois word for a settlement

Carinthia *(1925-1940)* the southernmost province of Austria, once part of the Hapsburg Empire

Catalonia *(1881-1901)* called after the region of Spain whose capital is Barcelona

Cephalonia *(1882-1901)* the Greek island named after the legendary Kephalos, banished from Athens for murdering his wife

China *(1862-1880)* a Sanskrit rather than Chinese word, first used in Europe by Marco Polo to refer to the area he had explored

Columbia *(1841-1843)* chosen by Samuel Cunard to honour the discoverer of the country where his port of Boston was located

Etruria *(1885-1910)* the area of Northern Italy inhabited by the Etruscans whose civilisation long predated the Romans

Europa *(1848-1867)* the continent called after a Phoenician princess with whom the Greek god Zeus fell in love

R.M.S "ETRURIA,"

CAPT. HENRY WALKER. (Lieut. R.N.R.)

Cuba *(1864-1876)* originally named Joanna by Christopher Columbus, although the present name comes from the native Cubanascnan

Damascus *(1860-1912)* the capital of Syria and the world's oldest, continuously inhabited city

Etna *(1855-1881)* named after Mount Etna in Sicily, Europe's highest volcano

Feltria *(1916-1917)* a Roman town in the Veneto region of Italy

Franconia *(1911-1916)* the kingdom of the Franks, the German tribe after which France is called

Gallia *(1879-1897)* the Roman province of Gaul, modern-day France

R.M.S

"*Franconia*"

Hecla *(1860-1881)* named after Mount Hecla in Iceland, one of the world's most active volcanoes

Hibernia *(1843-1850)* a Roman name for Ireland

Ivernia *(1900-1916)* another ancient name for Ireland

Java *(1865-1878)* one of the 17,508 islands of Indonesia whose capital Jakarta was named Batavia by the Dutch in 1619

Jura *(1857-1878)* the European mountain range separating France and Switzerland

Karnak *(1855-1862)* the Egyptian temple complex, the largest ever built

Kedar *(1860-1897)* named after the nomadic Bedouin tribes of north west Arabia who traced their lineage back to Abraham

Laconia *(1912-1917)* the region of southern Greece where the Spartans lived

Lancastria *(1922-1940)* the town on the river Lune in north west England where the Romans had a camp

Lebanon *(1855-1859)* the Near Eastern land of the Canaanites, whom the Greeks called Phoenicians after the purple dye they traded

Lucania *(1893-1909)* the region of Southern Italy, first settled by the Lyki from Anatolia 500 years before the Greeks invaded

Lusitania *(1907-1915)* the Roman province corresponding to modern Portugal

Malta *(1866-1889)* the group of Mediterranean islands which St Paul converted to Christianity

Marathon *(1861-1889)* the Greek town which gave its name to a battle and a race

Mauretania *(1907-1935)* the Roman province corresponding to modern Morocco and Algeria

Media *(1947-1961)* an ancient empire, conquered by the Persians in Biblical times

Melita *(1853-1868)* the island in the Mediterranean known today as Malta

"*MAURETANIA*"

Cunard
White Star

Niagara *(1848-1866)* celebrating the Niagara Falls linking two of the countries that were key to Samuel Cunard's success

Olympus *(1860-1881)* Greece's highest mountain and legendary home of the gods

Oregon *(1884-1886)* bought by Cunard from the Guion Line who named many of its ships after American States

Palestine *(1860-1862)* the region of the eastern Mediterranean called after the Plesheth or Philistine tribes

Palmyra *(1866-1896)* the ancient Syrian city on the silk road to China

Pannonia *(1904-1922)* the Roman province around the Danube

Parthia *(1870-1883)* the super power which ruled most of the Middle East and south west Asia in classical times

Pavonia possibly named after the land opposite Manhattan, named Pavonia after its owner Mynheer Paauw in 1624

Persia *(1856-1872)* the ancient Empire that once stretched from Pakistan to the Mediterranean

Russia *(1867-1880)* named after a Viking warlord, Rurik, who settled in Novgorod and named the area 'the land of the oarsmen'

Samaria *(1869-1896)* the Roman province on the west bank of the Jordan

Saragossa *(1874-1880)* the Spanish province named in honour of Caesar Augustus. The Arabs later called it Saragusta

Saxonia *(1900-1925)* the Roman name for the region of Germany still called Saxony today

Scotia *(1862-1879)* an ancient name for Ireland, possibly derived from its Egyptian royal ancestor Scota

Scythia *(1875-1898)* the region to the north and north east of the Black Sea whose inhabitants were the first to ride horses

R·M·S

"SCYTHIA"

Servia *(1881-1902)* modern Serbia, named by the tribe who invaded it in the 7th century AD

Siberia *(1867-1880)* the icy vastness east of the Urals named 'the calm lands' by the Mongols

Sidon *(1863-1885)* Lebanon's third largest city and the ancient capital of the Phoenicians

Slavonia *(1904-1909)* a region of north east Croatia, one of several named after Slav tribes

Tarifa *(1865-1898)* the town at the south west tip of Spain that faces both the Atlantic and the Mediterranean

Teneriffe *(1854-1859)* the largest of the Canary islands believed by seafarers to be the remains of the legendary city of Atlantis

Transylvania *(1914-1917)* a region of Romania named in Latin 'the land beyond the forest' around 1000AD

Tripoli *(1865-1872)* one of the three cities of the area of Libya known by the Romans as Tripolitania

Tuscania *(1915-1918)* the name of the Etruscan tribe who settled in the Tuscany region of Italy about 1000 BC

Ultonia *(1898-1917)* named by Roman writers as the area corresponding to modern Northern Ireland

Umbria *(1884-1910)* the Roman name for a region of central Italy

CUNARD TIME
Cunard Line's first century

1838 The Admiralty invites tenders for 'the conveyance of the Atlantic mails'.

1839 Samuel Cunard establishes the British and North American Steam Packet Company.

1840 Britannia sets out on her maiden voyage on American Independence Day.

1841 The Columbia breaks the west-bound speed record.

1842 Author Charles Dickens crosses on the Britannia.

1843 Cunard experiences its first serious accident when the Columbia is wrecked.

1844 The Britannia is stuck fast in the ice in Boston Harbor.

1845 Founding partner David McIver dies and is replaced by his brother Charles.

1846 The Acadia takes ether to Britain, after its first ever use for anesthesia in Boston.

1847 The Hibernia becomes the first Cunarder to sail into New York Harbor.

1848 The fleet is doubled with the America, Niagara, Europa and Canada.

1849 The Canada takes the eastbound speed record.

1850 The Collins Line's Atlantic ushers in an era of serious competition.

1851 Cunarders carry Americans to London for the Great Exhibition.

1852 The Andes is Cunard's first iron-hulled vessel.

1853 The Alps sets out on her maiden voyage.

1854 Eleven Cunard ships are requisitioned for the Crimean War.

1855 Sea lanes are introduced on the Atlantic to reduce the risk of collisions.

1856 The coal-guzzling Persia becomes the largest ship on the Atlantic.

1857 Cunard's growing business moves to larger headquarters in Liverpool.

1858 Fellow Cunarders the Europa and the Arabia collide.

1859 Samuel Cunard is knighted by Queen Victoria.

1860 It cost £8 to cross the Atlantic in steerage class.

1861 Two Cunarders ferry troops and supplies to Canada during the Trent incident.

1862 The China is Cunard's first ship with accommodation specifically for emigrants.

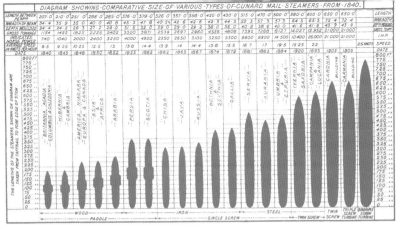

Above Comparing the Carmania with previous Cunarders, 1905.

1863 Following a heart attack Samuel Cunard hands over the reins to his sons.

1864 After being sold by Cunard the Arabia is converted into a sailing ship.

1865 Sir Samuel Cunard dies at the age of 78.

1866 Britain and North America are finally linked by telegraph cable.

1867 Cunarders stop making regular calls at Halifax, Nova Scotia.

1868 The Hibernia is lost at sea, after serving with the Spanish navy from 1850.

1869 During the next 41 years Robert Bell will be chief engineer on eight Cunarders.

1870 Competitor White Star Line launches the Oceanic, the first 'travelling palace'.

1871 Farmer's son Henri Arnoldy emigrates on the Algeria to start 'a new life'.

1872 It was 'rather safer to be on board their vessels than on the shore.' (Mark Twain)

1873 Future Commodore James 'Foggy' Watt joins Cunard.

1874 The Bothnia has the first dedicated smoking room at sea.

1875 The Scythia breaks a propeller after colliding with a whale.

1876 The Board disagree over introduction of 'extra frills' to compete with White Star.

1877 Emigrant Ladies are advised to 'Say au revoir cheerfully and bravely.'

1878 Cunard becomes a public company - Cunard Steamship Limited.

1879 The Gallia makes her maiden voyage, the first Cunarder to look like a liner.

1880 The Batavia's trial run to Bombay is Cunard's only venture into the Eastern trade.

1881 The Servia, Cunard's first steel vessel, is the world's first ship with electricity.
1882 The first known example of a ship's newspaper is published on the Parthia.
1883 The Aurania is the first liner to be fitted with suites of rooms.
1884 The Umbria and Etruria are the last Atlantic passenger ships to carry sail.
1885 The Etruria captures the westbound speed record.
1886 Passengers consume an egg a minute on an average crossing on the Etruria.
1887 The Umbria takes the westbound speed record from the Etruria.
1888 By his death the Etruria's designer is planning a ship that can cross in five days.
1889 The Malta is wrecked off Land's End without loss of life.
1890 Journalists first use the term 'Blue Riband of the North Atlantic'.
1891 In the next two decades 1.8m people will emigrate to Canada, many on Cunarders.
1892 Ellis Island opens as New York's immigration station.
1893 The Campania is the first twin-screw Cunarder.
1894 The Campania wins the Blue Riband for Cunard.
1895 The Sylvania makes her maiden voyage as a Cunard Atlantic cargo vessel.
1896 Samuel's great granddaughter, writer and socialite Nancy Cunard, is born.
1897 The Gallia, which crossed in seven days in 1886, ends her career with Cunard.
1898 Built as a cattle boat, the Ultonia will carry 2100 third class passengers by 1904.
1899 The Saxonia sets out, graced with the world's tallest funnel.
1900 Ships' orchestras are starting to tune up on the liners.
1901 The Lucania is the first Cunarder fitted with Marconi's wireless telegraph.
1902 Eight Cunarders carry 75,000 troops, refugees and prisoners during the Boer War.
1903 The Government provides support for two super-liners if Cunard remains British.
1904 The wife of the US Ambassador to Britain launches the Caronia.
1905 Cunard tests out steam turbine technology on the Carmania.
1906 Glass from the champagne bottle launching the Mauretania injures a workman.
1907 Sister super-liner Lusitania sets out on her maiden voyage.
1908 Lucy holds on to the Blue Riband.
1909 Sister Maury steals it from her and retains it until 1929.

1910 The Carmania, Caronia and Franconia offer Mediterranean cruises.

1911 The Franconia has the first on-board gymnasium.

1912 On 15th April Carpathia rescues over 700 survivors from White Star Line's Titanic.

1913 The Aquitania is launched, the first Cunarder with an indoor swimming pool.

1914 The outbreak of World War I interrupts normal service.

1915 The Lusitania is torpedoed off Ireland with the loss of over 1200 lives.

1916 Cunard plans to switch to oil burning for its post-war fleet.

1917 The Cunard Building on Liverpool's Pier Head is completed.

1918 Cunard has carried over 1m troops and 10m tons of cargo during the War.

1919 Cunard receives the German liner Imperator to compensate for the Lusitania.

1920 The Imperator is renamed Berengaria after the wife of Richard the Lion Heart.

1921 On the Aquitania 'emigrants rough it in comfort, cleanliness and warmth.'

1922 Government slashes the number of immigrants allowed into the USA.

1923 The Laconia sets off on the first-ever world cruise.

1924 The Tyrrhenia (1922) becomes the Lancastria: the public disliked her original name.

1925 Cunard takes delivery of the last of nine new passenger liners since 1918.

1926 Cunard carries more passengers across the Atlantic than any other line.

1927 The Carinthia breaks wireless records, making contact over 12,000 miles.

1928 Early experiments in television take place on the Berengaria.

1929 Passengers playing the Berengaria Stock Exchange learn of the Great Crash.

1930 The keel for Job No. 534 is laid.

1931 3000 men are laid off just before Christmas when Job No. 534 is cancelled.

1932 The Carmania is broken up for scrap in the depths of the Depression.

1933 The great liners take to weekend cruises to earn money.

1934 Cunard merges with White Star and the Queen Mary is finally launched.

1935 The Aquitania uses 1000 gallons of paint and varnish to keep shipshape.

1936 The Queen Mary sets off on her maiden voyage.

1937 The Cunard-White Star Line lays down Job No. 1029, the future Mauretania II.

1938 As war clouds gather, the Queen Elizabeth, the world's largest liner is launched.

BUILDING A QUEEN
Shipyard workers' memories of the Queen Mary

From 1899 John Brown's shipyard in Clydebank, Scotland built 17 Cunard liners including the Lusitania, Aquitania and three of the Queens. The most famous job of all was No. 534 – the future Queen Mary. During the depths of the Depression work was halted for 18 months on 534. Her rusting hull towering over the town became a national icon of despair and then of hope when work restarted at Easter, 1934.

'We worried about how we would stand up to hard work after such a long time idle.'

Building the Queen Mary was dirty, deafening and dangerous. Men worked a 47.5 hour week and rest facilities were primitive:

'A ship is such an awkward thing: a great big lump of steel – it's so unrelenting, unyielding. You've put it through the furnace: you've done everything to try and shape it: to impose your will on that steel.'

'I've seen us wi' a heavy job, working the punch wi' the sweat blinding ye and the icicles hanging to the machines.'

Boys left school at 14 to sign on as apprentices.

'The foreman took one look at my short trousers and told me to go home and get a pair of long trousers and come back in the afternoon. And so I went home and my mother made me a pair of trousers out of an old coat.'

'I was stuck in the bowels of the ship. I couldnae believe it: they were throwing red hot rivets to each other. It was dark and stinking because of the oil lamps they used. I thought it was Hell.'

On 26th September the men who had built her lined both sides of the river Clyde as the Queen Mary slipped into the water.

'Men would be riveting 80 to 100 ft up, swinging hammers on two wooden planks, sometimes only one, without any guard rail.'

'When the order book was full, the pubs were full.'

'The boy throws the hot rivet to the holder-on and he picks up the hot rivet, sparking hot, and rams it through the hole with a back-hammer. The riveter drives it in with alternate blows on the outside of the shell.'

Over ten million red-hot rivets had to be hammered in to hold the plates of the liner's hull together.

'The foreman would walk up and down the lines of men waiting for work without saying a word, not even a grunt. That meant there was no work for you that day. They were just reminding you that they had all the power and you had none.'

'The toilets were just a running trough. A favourite trick was for somebody to set fire to a ball of newspaper and float it down the line of 'busy' men. Then you'd hear the howls as the men jumped to their feet.'

'I NAME THIS SHIP'

The launch of a new liner was a red letter day in Cunard's calendar

When the Caronia was launched in 1905, one English wit commented: 'She's that big you'd think they wanted a brewery of champagne to christen her.'

In 1906 the convoy of new-fangled cars, carrying the dignitaries from lunch to the launch, drove two abreast through three of the Mauretania's four funnels laid end to end.

It has always been considered bad luck for a man to christen a ship. In 1912 Kaiser Wilhelm II decided to defy tradition and, wearing the uniform of a German admiral, named the world's largest passenger ship Imperator. After the defeat of Germany in the First World War, Cunard inherited the liner in compensation for the loss of the Lusitania. Renamed Berengaria, she became the flagship of the fleet.

The tradition of royal christenings began on 26th September, 1934 when Queen Mary christened the Queen Mary. After a speech by King George V, the Queen stepped forward and whispered 'Which buttons do I press?' With a pair of golden scissors, she cut the pink ribbon that sent a bottle of

Australian wine shattering against the liner's bow. As the new Queen slipped into the Clyde, the Queen turned to her husband and asked 'Was that right?'

On 27th September, 1938 Queen Elizabeth launched her namesake into the river Clyde. Although King George VI was detained in London by the Munich crisis, the Queen was joined by the Princesses Elizabeth and Margaret. The Managing Director of John Brown's shipyard had to cut the Queen's speech short when the vessel started to move down the slipway: 'Ma'am she's going. Launch her please.'

Attended by the Duke of Edinburgh and Princess Margaret, the Queen launched the Queen Elizabeth 2 on 20th September, 1967. She used the same pair of gold scissors as her mother and grandmother when launching the first two Queens. The Managing Director

of John Brown's shipyard vetoed Cunard's suggestion of approaching the Beatles to write and perform a song for the occasion. Instead he invited a local pipe band to play 'Scotland the Brave'.

Princess Grace of Monaco, the former film star Grace Kelly, christened the Cunard Princess in New York in 1977. A second mother and daughter christening was celebrated when Princess Caroline of Monaco named Sea Goddess 2 in 1986.

'I name this ship Queen Mary 2. May God bless her and all who sail in her.' On 8th January, 2004, the Queen reverted to the tradition of breaking a bottle of French champagne over the bow. She pulled a lever to release the arm which held the bottle. The arm was programmed to hit a spike welded on the hull resulting in a foam of bubbles.

SEASICK ALL DAY
'Not ill but going to be'

In 1842 Charles Dickens described what was an all too common experience for passengers crossing the North Atlantic, one of the world's wildest oceans. On an average crossing a fifth of passengers could be confined to their cabins and even seasoned crew were not immune.

A few stalwarts revelled in rough seas. One New York businessman commented of the Parthia (1948), a notoriously unstable ship: 'I really feel I've been to sea on this old cow. On the Queens you might as well be on Central Park Lake.'

Each liner had its own reputation. The Mauretania and Lusitania were famous for their swoop and dive when their bows could lift 60 ft. According to her crew the Queen Mary could roll the milk out of a cup of tea, On one crossing of the Carinthia II (1925), so much crockery was broken that the stewards had to serve hot drinks in paper cups.

Right From the mid 1950s, stabilisers provided a much smoother crossing on the Queen Mary.

Joseph Maguire, doctor on the Queens in the 1950s admitted defeat: 'I have been asked times without number if there is a certain cure for this distressing malady. If I knew that answer, I might have retired years ago, one of the richest men in the world. Some cures help some people - that's all I can say.'

Cures were legion. The traditions of deck games and a cup of the clear soup, bouillon, served on deck at 11am, were introduced partly as a way of avoiding seasickness. In the 1890s Cunard recommended lager as an excellent preventative although ice cream was to be avoided at all costs. Individual passengers swore by remedies from raw celery, baked potatoes and avoiding jam, to rum with grapefruit juice or a pint of champagne.

Tips were not confined to food. 'Only those who have experienced the struggles of the dressing hour when seasick, know what ludicrous importance every button, tie or hairpin assumes.' Queasy diners were advised to choose a table near the door as 'Seasickness is a wonderful training for sprinters.'

CUNARD TO THE RESCUE

Fire, fog, submerged rocks and storms were no respecters of ships on the Atlantic

A shout from the look-out on the crow's nest, an SOS picked up by the wireless operator or the cry of 'Man overboard' sent Cunarders steaming to the rescue.

Author Mark Twain was a passenger on the Batavia in 1872 when 'at 4 pm a dismasted vessel was sighted. A furious squall had just broken upon us, and the sea was running mountains high. Nevertheless Captain Mouland immediately bore up for the wreck, which was making signals of distress, ordered out a life-boat, and called for volunteers. To a landsman it seemed like deliberate suicide to go out in such a storm, but our third and fourth officers and eight men answered the call with a promptness that compelled a cheer. We could see nine men clinging to the main rigging. The stern of the vessel was gone, and the sea made a clean breach over her, pouring in a cataract out of the broken stern, and spouting through the parted planks of her bows. 'All nine men were rescued and the Batavia resumed her course.

In September 1910 passengers lined the decks of the Mauretania to watch the dramatic rescue of the captain of the Liverpool steamer West Point and 15 of his crew. They had been forced to abandon ship in mid-Atlantic after a devastating fire. When their lifeboat was sighted the great liner turned and steamed to their aid, the rescue operation taking 48 minutes despite

Above Contemporary newspaper illustration showing the postion of the Titanic and other nearby ships.

atrocious seas. While the injured captain of the West Point was receiving medical attention, a bedraggled white kitten leapt out from inside his shirt. Passengers bid for the privilege of keeping the ship's cat Omar, the funds raised going to the crew of the stricken ship.

In October 1913 the Carmania was on her way from New York to Liverpool, when she received an SOS from the emigrant ship Volturno that she was ablaze. Four hours later, the Carmania reached the stricken ship carrying 657 passengers and crew but was forced to stand by during the night because of atrocious weather. As dawn broke, she managed to pick up over 500 survivors including many Russian Jewish emigrants. Captain James Barr and his crew were presented with an award for gallantry.

The most famous rescue of all was made by the Carpathia on 15th April, 1912 after her wireless officer picked up a distress signal from the Titanic, the liner that was rumoured to be unsinkable. Captain Arthur Rostron modestly described his part in the ensuing drama: "We steamed at full speed and did what we could. … Some other Hand than mine was on that helm during the night.' Despite never having had to respond to an emergency call in his

many years at sea, he spared no effort in preparing the ship, from rigging ropes and nets for survivors to clamber up to ordering hot drinks for his crew in readiness for the long night ahead. At 9am the last of the 703 survivors out of the 2206 passengers and crew of the Titanic stepped aboard the Carpathia.

Six weeks after the Titanic disaster, Molly Brown presented a silver loving cup to Captain Rostron, on behalf of the survivors, all of whom had been rescued by the Carpathia. Survivors also raised money to present medals to the Cunarder's gallant crew.

Drama at sea can arise when cruising as well as crossing. While sailing in the Caribbean in January 1971 the QE2 received an SOS call from the French liner Antilles which had run aground. Leaking fuel oil caught fire and by the time the QE2 reached her the Antilles was an inferno. Fortunately the passengers had already been safely ferried by lifeboat to the island of Mustique where the QE2 and two French ships picked them up.

CUNARD FIRST
Innovation on the liners

Samuel Cunard preferred to use proven technology rather than put passengers at risk. Although the shipping line has remained true to his principle of safety over speed, it has achieved many firsts over the last 160 years.

The **Britannia** (1840) was the first trans-Atlantic mail carrier and the first ship to run to a regular time-table.

In 1847 the **America, Niagara, Europa** and **Canada** became the first ships to use navigation lights at night: port red, starboard green, and foremasthead white.

The **Arabia** (1852) had the first onboard nursery and the Bothnia (1874) the first smoking room.

The **Servia** (1881) was the first ship in the world to be built with an electricity supply. She was also Cunard's first steel ship and its first to rely solely on passenger income.

The '**Parthia Evening Post**' of 11th September, 1882 is the first known example of a ship's newspaper.

The **Aurania** (1883) was the first liner fitted with suites of rooms.

The **Campania** (1893) and **Lucania** (1893) were the first Atlantic liners to have refrigeration machinery.

In 1903 the **Lucania** published the first daily news bulletin at sea. The front page headline of Issue 1 was 'Signor Marconi on Board.'

The first mid-Atlantic chess game was played between the **Etruria** and the US vessel Philadelphia in 1903.

The **Caronia** (1905) had the first room named 'Lounge'.

The 15th century style lift grilles on the **Mauretania** represented the first use of aluminium in marine applications.

The **Franconia** (1911) was the world's first ship to have a gymnasium. Passengers also enjoyed a Verandah Café and a sun deck for the first time. She was the first large liner to have hot and cold water in every cabin.

The **Aquitania** (1914) had the world's first onboard indoor swimming pool.

On war service in 1915 the **Campania** became the first Royal Navy vessel to launch aircraft while under way.

In January 1923 the **Laconia** set out on the first ever world cruise.

In 1924 Cunard was the first shipping company to introduce **tourist third class,** to bring Atlantic travel within the reach of everyone.

In 1928 the **Berengaria** set a new wireless record by handling 50,640 words excluding press messages on one crossing.

The **Queen Mary** was the world's first ship planned from the start to have an onboard church, chapel and synagogue. She was also the first British ship to have a safe deposit.

In 1934 the **Queen Mary** was the first international passenger ship to be launched by a member of the royal family. It was also the first time that a ship launch was broadcast on radio.

The **Media** (1947) was the first Atlantic liner to make a truly smooth crossing, thanks to her revolutionary fin stabilisers.

The **Caronia II** (1949) was the first liner specifically designed as a cruise ship.

In 1982 the **QE2** became the world's largest hospital ship when transporting injured troops from the Falklands War.

In July 1986 the first satellite transmission of a TV programme from a merchant ship at sea went out from the **QE2**. In the same year the first seagoing branch of Harrods opened.

Queen Mary 2 (2004) has the first floating Planetarium and the longest jogging track at sea. The 'Queen Mary 2' signs near her funnel are the largest illuminated ship's name signs in maritime history.

'HUMAN AUDACITY IN STEEL'

Feats of naval engineering

This was how Cunard's Chairman Percy Bates described the Queen Mary. In their battle against the forces of the North Atlantic, leviathan liners demanded immensely strong hulls and gigantic pieces of machinery.

The **Aquitania's** steel rudder was 70 tons, half the weight of the world's heaviest animal, the great blue whale.

The propulsion of the **Aquitania's** turbines equalled the heave of five million Roman galley slaves.

Each of the **Queen Mary's** four, 30 ton screw propellers were mounted so precisely that they could be turned by a man's hand. Women were banned from the shipyard in case they distracted the fitters.

Placed end to end, the ten million rivets which held the **Queen Elizabeth's** hull together could stretch from Boston to New York.

The **Mauretania II's** 14.6 ft gear wheels were the largest ever cast. The 500 teeth on each

wheel were cast to a precision of 100,000th of an inch.

The cable of the **Mauretania II** was a third of a mile long and weighed 96 tons. Each of her three anchors weighed 9.75 tons.

Each of the **QE2's** nine diesel electric engines is the size of a double-decker bus.

Over 900 miles of welding fuse together the thousands of units that make up **Queen Mary 2**.

Queen Mary 2 is one of the largest manmade objects ever built that move under their own power. Her engines produce the thrust to maintain three Boeing 747s cruising at 530 miles per hour.

Below and right Measuring up to the scale of the Mauretania II (1939).

Left WW1 survivor Mauretania in her camouflage coat of dazzle paint.

'LEST WE FORGET'

Cunarders lost in the World Wars

Cunarders and their crew played a vital role in both World Wars, ferrying troops, supplies, the wounded and prisoners-of-war. Many did not return.

WW I	7th May, 1915	**Lusitania**	Torpedoed and sunk. *1,201 lives lost.*
	4th October, 1916	**Franconia**	Torpedoed and sunk. *12 lives lost.*
	19th October, 1916	**Alaunia**	Mined and sunk. *Two lives lost.*
	1st January, 1917	**Ivernia**	Torpedoed and sunk. *121 lives lost.*
	25th February, 1917	**Laconia**	Torpedoed and sunk. *12 lives lost.*
	11th March, 1917	**Folia**	Torpedoed and sunk, *11 lives lost.*
	4th May, 1917	**Transylvania**	Torpedoed and sunk. *414 lives lost.*
	5th May, 1917	**Feltria**	Torpedoed and sunk. *45 lives lost.*
	27th June, 1917	**Ultonia**	Torpedoed and sunk. *One life lost.*
	27th January, 1918	**Andania**	Torpedoed and sunk. *Seven lives lost.*
	4th February, 1918	**Aurania II**	Torpedoed and sunk. *Nine lives lost.*
	30th May, 1918	**Ausonia**	Torpedoed and sunk. *44 lives lost.*
	13th June, 1918	**Ascania**	Wrecked. *No lives lost.*
	18th July, 1918	**Carpathia**	Torpedoed and sunk. *Five lives lost.*
	24th August, 1918	**Flavia**	Torpedoed and sunk. *One life lost.*
	5th November, 1918	**Campania**	Sunk in collision. *No lives lost.*
WW II	6th June, 1940	**Carinthia**	Torpedoed and sunk. *Four lives lost.*
	16th June, 1940	**Andania**	Torpedoed and sunk. *No lives lost.*
	17th June, 1940	**Lancastria II**	Bombed and sunk. *5,000-9,000 lives lost.*
	4th November, 1940	**Laurentic**	Torpedoed and sunk. *49 lives lost.*
	12th September, 1942	**Laconia II**	Torpedoed and sunk. *2,275 lives lost.*

WHO'S FOR DECK TENNIS?

Games played on board

Deck games arose as a way of exercising and of passing the time on late 19th century liners. On the Queen Mary the area laid out for deck games was the equivalent of the football pitch at Wembley. By the 1980s Cunard claimed that it would take a passenger four months to experience all of the QE2's on-board activities.

Popular deck games have included:

Croquet Played as early as the 1860s, deck croquet used flat wooden pucks instead of balls and rings marked on the deck instead of hoops.

Deck quoits The quoits were usually thrown over a brass spike set into the deck but could also be thrown into a bucket or lobbed over spikes on an inclined board.

Deck tennis Also known as tennequoits or tennikoit, deck tennis was a hybrid of tennis and quoits involving tossing a small rope ring or rubber quoit back and forth over a net.

Right Quoits on the deck of the Franconia II (1923).

Mini-golf This was played with shuffleboard equipment over a course of chalked-in and real life hazards from stanchions to deck chairs. The Aquitania also had a putting green.

Shuffleboard

Two-four players took turns to slide discs with a cue onto a target area chalked or later painted on the deck. Each square represented a different number of points, the winner being the first player to achieve a score of 50 or 100.

```
      +10
  6    1    8
  7    5    3
  2    9    4
      -10
```

Squash Although squash courts with an attendant to give passengers a game were introduced on the Queens in the early 1950s, it never caught on as a deck game.

Passengers and crew also devised some more unusual deck entertainments, including:

Biscuit and whistle race The winner was the first to whistle a recognisable tune through a mouthful of dry biscuit.
Blind man's bottle Women steered their reined and blindfolded partners round a course of bottles.
Cigarette and needle race The man threaded a needle while his partner puffed away.
Deck chess Played on a giant board.
Dog dressing up shows
Egg and spoon races
Fancy dress or **hat competitions**
Four-legged races With three players
Giant Holo The player had to coax a ball through a tunnel with a stick.
Horse racing The real fun was in the betting on the toy horses.
Leap frog races
Marking the pig's eye A variation of pinning the tail on the donkey.
Obstacle races Players dressed up in a series of unlikely garments from a suitcase in the fastest time.
Pillow fights Between two men perched astride a pole.

Pole wrestling Over a sail filled with water.
Prize fights Between crew members.
Skipping races
Spiro-ball or **Bubble-Puppy** A kind of tennis solitaire.
Three-legged races
Tug of war contests On one Cunarder in 1924 'The Merry Widows' tested their strength against 'The Merry Widowers'
Wheelbarrow races With a passenger with roller skates on their hands being the barrow.

Right Blindfold race on the Queen Mary.
Below A boxing match on the Queen Mary.

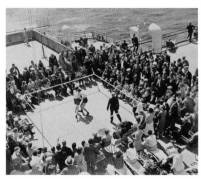

TWENTY DO'S AND DON'TS
Steward etiquette

Shipping companies and training schools produced guidance on how to become a good steward. Advice included:

Do   Remember that oysters are the exception to the rule of forks to the left and knives to the right
Find out in advance of serving what snowflake salad or potage Jackson is
Always serve from the left
Remove nicotine stains on your hands with a pumice stone
'When serving passengers, turn slightly away and retain the breath as much as possible'
Keep your hands out of your pockets
Speak to passengers only when spoken to
Confine conversation with stewardesses to work-related topics
'Think more and walk less. A little forethought may save an enormous amount of energy'
'Restrain outward expression of annoyance even under the most trying circumstances'

Don't Smoke while on duty
Fall asleep in a passenger cabin while cleaning it
Wear scent or hair oil
'Run, push or indulge in any kind of horse play'
Converse with other stewards in the presence of passengers
Fraternise with passengers of the opposite sex
Return to the ship drunk after an evening's shore leave
Use a passenger lavatory, however urgent the need
Peek into a passenger bathroom when in use: the penalty - instant dismissal
Disobey an officer's orders

'As a general rule advance comes more rapidly to those who have, in addition to the indispensable qualities of deftness, quickness, civility, and a certain measure of refinement of speech and manner, cleanliness in both person and work, a natural aptitude to desire and please, a cheerful, pleasant manner, endless patience and sufficient self-control.'

Do's and Don'ts for Stewards

'It is easier to fit a square peg into a round hole than to mould into a good steward a person of slow intellect, disobliging and tactless disposition, heavy movements, bad manners or a raucous voice.'

How to Obtain Berths on the Large Liners, 1904

THE FOUNDING FATHERS

Cunard, Napier, Burns and the McIvers

As a boy **Samuel Cunard** loved to watch sailing ships bringing the mail from Europe into the port of Halifax. When the successful Nova Scotian merchant later visited England, he experienced the speed and efficiency of the new steam railway. It set him dreaming of 'an ocean railway'. In 1838 he noticed a newspaper advertisement placed by the British Admiralty for a fortnightly Atlantic mail service. With the contract in his pocket less than three months later, Samuel urgently needed ships and money. He found backers in Glasgow, Scotland's mercantile capital on the river Clyde.

Robert Napier was a Glasgow blacksmith who was fascinated by the new technology of steam. In 1827 he made his reputation when boats with Napier engines took the first two places in a steam yacht race on the Clyde. He too dreamed of setting up a steamship service across the Atlantic. He persuaded Samuel to build larger and more powerful ships than specified in the Royal Mail contract, even offering to reduce his share of the profits in order to help finance them.

Robert Napier introduced Samuel to ship owners **George** and **James Burns**. Their experience of carrying the mail to Liverpool and Northern Ireland told them that Samuel was on to a winner. George became the first Chairman of the British and North American Royal Mail Steam Packet Company, the cumbersome title that the public soon shortened to Cunard.

Robert Napier also introduced Samuel to **David** and **Charles McIver**, the Glasgow businessmen who had moved to Liverpool to rum a steamship service across the Irish Sea. Although at first reluctant to risk their money, the brothers were won round by Robert to invest in the great venture. In the early 1850s they developed Cunard's passenger and freight Mediterranean services.

And so a shipping line was born, making its founders wealthy men.

Above George Burns.

Above Charles McIver.

BUILT BY
The shipyards that launched Cunarders

All Cunarders have been built in Europe. Three quarters of those commissioned before 1950 were launched on the river Clyde in Scotland. Orders from the shipping line helped 'Clyde-built' to become a synonym for quality.

ALSTOM Chantiers de l'Atlantique, Nantes, France
2003   Queen Mary 2

Armstrong Whitworth, Newcastle, England
1921   Ausonia II
1923   Ascania II

Barclay, Curle & Co, Glasgow, Scotland
1912   Czar

William Beardmore & Co Ltd, Clydebank, Scotland
1919   Cameronia II
1920   Lancastria

Blohm & Voss, Hamburg, Germany
1914   Majestic

John Brown's, Clydebank, Scotland
1899   Saxonia
1902   Pannonia
1904   Caronia
1905   Carmania
1906   Lusitania
1913   Aquitania
1922   Franconia II
1925   Alaunia II
1934   Queen Mary
1938   Queen Elizabeth
1946   Media

1947   Caronia II
1954   Saxonia II
1955   Carinthia III
1955   Ivernia II
1956   Sylvania II
1967   Queen Elizabeth 2

Burmeister Wain Skilos, Copenhagen, Denmark
1974   Cunard Countess
1975   Cunard Princess

Caird & Co, Greenock, Scotland
1854   Etna
1865   Palmyra

Top ALSTOM workers on Queen Mary 2.

Right Johns Brown's shipyard.

Cammell Laird,
Birkenhead, England
1920   Samaria II
1938   Mauretania II

De Merwede van Vliet & Co,
Hardinxveld, Netherlands
1959   Prinses Irene

Alexander Denny,
Dumbarton, Scotland
1853   Melita

William Denny & Bros,
Dumbarton, Scotland
1849   British Queen
1852   Alps
1852   Andes
1852   Balbec

1853   Karnak
1853   Taurus
1853   Teneriffe
1856   Damascus
1860   Kedar
1861   Sidon
1870   Batavia
1870   Parthia
1891   Feltria

Robert Duncan,
Greenock, Scotland
1840   Britannia

John Elder & Co,
Glasgow, Scotland
1883   Oregon
1884   Etruria
1884   Umbria

Fairfield Shipbuilding,
Glasgow, Scotland
1892   Campania
1893   Lucania
1907   Royal George
1921   Tuscania II
1922   Athenia
1925   Letitia

Harland & Wolff, Belfast,
Northern Ireland
1910   Olympic
1913   Orduna
1927   Laurentic
1929   Britannic III
1931   Georgic
1947   Parthia II

All images Cammell Laird, Birkenhead.

Hawthorn Leslie & Co,
Newcastle, England
1921   Andania II

D & W Henderson Ltd,
Glasgow, Scotland
1907   California
1911   Cameronia

Hollming Oy,
Rauma, Finland
1985   Sea Goddess II

Sir J Laing & Sons,
Sunderland, England
1902   Slavonia

Laird Bros,
Birkenhead, England
1882   Cephalonia

London & Glasgow Co,
Glasgow, Scotland
1895   Sylvania

Robert Napier & Sons,
Glasgow, Scotland
1853   Emeu
1856   Persia
1860   Hecla

1861   China
1861   Marathon
1861   Scotia

Palmers Co Ltd,
Jarrow, England
1901   Flavia

Rotterdamsche Droogdok,
Rotterdam, Netherlands
1971   Cunard Adventurer
1972   Cunard Ambassador

F Schichau,
Danzig, Poland
1913   Homeric

Scott's of Greenock,
Greenock, Scotland
1906   Cassandra
1913   Alaunia
1913   Andania
1914   Transylvania
1920   Albania II

Soc des Forges de la Mediterranee,
La Seyne, France
1965   Sagafjord

Robert Steele & Co,
Greenock, Scotland
1840   Columbia
1842   Hibernia
1844   Cambria
1847   America
1847   Niagara
1848   Canada
1850   Africa
1850   Asia
1851   Arabia
1858   Palestine

Alexander Stephen & Sons,
Glasgow, Scotland
1914   Tuscania

Swan Hunter,
Newcastle, England
1898   Ultonia
1899   Ivernia
1900   Albania
1902   Carpathia
1906   Mauretania
1909   Ausonia
1910   Franconia
1911   Ascania
1911   Laconia
1916   Aurania II

1921	Laconia II
1924	Aurania III
1973	Caronia III

J & G Thomson,
Glasgow, Scotland

1854	Jura
1854	Lebanon
1857	Australasian
1860	Atlas
1860	Olympus
1863	Tripoli
1864	Aleppo
1865	Java
1865	Malta
1865	Tarifa
1867	Russia
1867	Siberia
1868	Samaria
1870	Abyssinia
1870	Algeria
1874	Bothnia
1874	Saragossa
1874	Scythia
1878	Gallia
1881	Catalonia
1881	Servia
1882	Aurania
1882	Pavonia

Tod & McGregor,
Glasgow, Scotland

| 1857 | Nemesis |
| 1864 | Cuba |

Union Naval de Levante,
Valencia, Spain

| 1989 | Crown Monarch |
| 1992 | Crown Jewel |

Vickers Ltd,
Barrow, England

1920	Scythia II
1921	Antonia
1925	Carinthia II

A G Vulcan,
Hamburg, Germany

| 1912 | Berengaria |

Wartsila,
Vaasa, Finland

1984	Sea Goddess I
1988	Royal Viking Sun
1993	Crown Dynasty

John Wood,
Port Glasgow, Scotland

| 1840 | Acadia |
| 1847 | Europa |

R Wood,
Port Glasgow, Scotland

| 1840 | Caledonia |

Workman, Clark & Co,
Belfast, Northern Ireland

| 1919 | Vauban |

Below Working on Job No.1029, the future Mauretania II at the Cammell Laird yard.

FOUR THREE TWO ONE
Funnel Facts

Since 1840 Cunard funnels have almost always been red and black. The original recipe for the red was achieved by mixing bright ochre and buttermilk which 'cooked' on to the hot smoke stacks: ordinary paint simply bubbled and peeled.

The Saxonia (*1899*) was unusual in having only one funnel. It was, however, the tallest in the world.

The funnels of the dashing **Campania** and **Lucania** of 1893 were raked backwards to enhance the impression of speed.

The funnels on the 1905 **Caronia** and **Carmania** were as high as the Eddystone lighthouse.

The **Lusitania** was the first four-funnel liner to have her stacks evenly spaced rather than being grouped in twos.

With her four gigantic funnels, the **Aquitania** was used by other ships as a measure of the thickness of fog. Its density was described a two-funnel, three-funnel or four-funnel.

Before the First World War, the number of funnels a liner had was seen as a status symbol. Travel agents could not persuade some clients to book on any ship with fewer than four.

When liners switched to oil burning, some funnels became redundant. Spare funnels were used as stores or crew restrooms.

Three large locomotives could fit into one of the **Queen Mary's** three funnels.

Above Franconia (1911) and Laconia (1912).

The Georgic *(1934)* had two funnels. When returned to service after being bombed and salvaged during the Second World War, she only had one.

The **Queen Elizabeth** had only two funnels to give her a more modern look than the **Queen Mary.**

The Caronia *(1949)* had one huge funnel - 46 ft high, 53 ft long and exactly half as wide.

The one exception to the black and red rule was the **QE2** whose white funnel with its revolutionary shape shocked traditionalists in 1969. She reverted to her old livery in the mid 1980s.

Despite appearances the **QE2** has two funnels. The gases from the engine and boiler rooms are vented out of the large funnel while the kitchens are vented through their own duct hidden in the forward mast.

Queen Mary 2 carries one of her namesake's whistles, the tone of whose deep bass A can be heard ten miles away.

Above right, top to bottom Lusitania (1907), Queen Mary (1936), Queen Elizabeth (1940), QE2 (1969).

IN THE HOLD
Unusual cargoes carried by Cunarders

Even express liners like the Queens carried a certain amount of cargo. It was usually made up of high value goods like animal skins or precious stones, or items like fashion magazines and perishable foods which had to travel quickly.

A typical cargo manifest for the Queen Elizabeth on a New York - Southampton crossing in 1951 included:

134 bundles of 'Collier's Magazine'
839 food gift parcels
1 carton of phono-records
The personal effects of a UK diplomat moving from New York to Moscow
A Pontiac sedan with 'extra wheel tyre, radio and seat covers'
A case of costume jewellery
Parts for IBM Ticketograph factory time recording machines
A case of blank American Express travellers' cheques
25 bars of silver bullion
A trunk of personal effects belonging to a Mr H. D. Martin of Cardiff
1 case of dental equipment
7 cases of artificial silk 'Junior Miss' briefs
3 bales of raw furs and 1 bale of raw Australian opossum skins
1 case of nylon hosiery
3 bales of raw skunk skins
Cans of film of the latest Hollywood movies
1 used tricycle and toy sword for Master Peter Baid
1 package of ship's log books
1 framed picture labelled 'not work of art' for the US Air Attache in London

Some more unusual cargoes carried by Cunarders have included:

Stage sets and drum kits for shows moving from London's West End to Broadway

'One tin box containing The Magna Carta' returned in 1946 after spending the War in New York for safekeeping

The first relic of the Buddha to be displayed in the USA – a piece of bone the size of a mustard seed – which travelled with a monk on the Queen Mary in 1955

A replica liberty torch carried on the QE2 as a gift from Cunard to the American nation as part of the Statue of Liberty centenary celebrations

Socialite Sir Bernard Docker's Rolls Royce with gold plated bumpers and wheel trim

A coracle, Welsh love-spoons, Lloyd George's walking stick, a harp and a model of a Welsh bible carved in anthracite by a Welsh miner, which accompanied Miss Wales on the Parthia in 1955

A 1910 Franklin, a 1914 Dodge, a 1911 Ford model T and a 1912 Abbott whose owners travelled on the QE2 in 1976 in a re-enactment of the legendary 1908 New York to Paris car race

Crates of whisky: the Parthia's main cargo in the 1950s. There were frequent 'breakages' in dock. Longshoremen were known to stand underneath cases marked 'damaged in handling' with a bucket to catch the drips.

Below Lowering a car to the mobile petrol station.

DRESSING FOR DINNER

Shipboard fashion through the years

With cramped cabins and communal dining, the first Cunard passengers dressed for a crossing that regularly involved being lashed by salt spray or showered with smuts from the smokestack.

'Accidents too and loss of life are possible at sea, and I have always felt that a body washed ashore in good clothes, would receive more respect and kinder care than if dressed in those only fit for the rag bag.'

Kate Ledoux, *Ocean Notes for Ladies*, 1877

From the late 19th century, however, people dressed to see and be seen in the new 'floating hotels'. Etiquette and fashion guides advised on what to wear and when. Even sailing day became a social occasion.

'There are pretty faces and handsome ones, fine figures and costumes that tempt the eye; men are smartly groomed and women exquisitely gowned. There is animation, even excitement, and a charming disregard for petty conventionalities. Not the opera, the ball, or the Horse Show, can equal the scene presented. ... There is a garden of bobbing millinery flowers, here a patch of violets and there of roses, and here and there and almost everywhere combinations of the fashionable colors, enlivened with the fluttering bits of white linen in tossing, waving hands. The effect is kaleidoscopic.'

John T. Maginnis, *New York Times Illustrated Magazine*, June 20, 1897.

Left Dressing for dinner on Scythia II (1921).

In 'An Aristocrat of the Atlantic' published about 1893, Maev 'a lady of fashion' advised women not to sit on their own on deck after dark. She also suggested that they wear heavy skirts and coloured rather than light petticoats on deck in case of embarrassing moments due to sea breezes: 'It is not unusual to dress in the evening for dinner ... dresses of serge will be found very serviceable.'

'The Mauretania and the Lusitania were the first Atlantic liners on which it was de rigueur to dress for dinner in first class. 'By day, Harris tweed ... Chanel jerseys ... indolent conversation, and energetic sport. By night a sudden increase in tempo, a blaze of jewels ... the gleam of ivory shoulders ... gowns, rose, gold, green ... men and women both wearing formal brilliance with the perfect ease that is the distinction and delight of aristocratic English life.'

Cunard publicity, Aquitania, 1914

'As for dinner dresses, remember the mistake made by the average American whether crossing for the first time or the twenty first time is to resemble the lily of the field with whom Solomon in all his glory refused to compete. Especially is this true on the return trip, where many otherwise excellent ladies try to wear each Parisian frock at least once to cheat the customs. To put it frankly, however, it simply isn't considered smart to appear too opulent. It subjects one to the suspicion of having nowhere else to wear one's clothes.'

Vogue, 1920s

Even the stewards were not immune to the glamour. 'I was able to study at close range the 1939 Glitterati in all their art deco era glory and finery. Elegant women in their long gowns with Mink and Fox draped over their pale English shoulders. A preponderance of long cigarette holders with smouldering De Reske or Turkish cigarettes proffered from gold and silver cigarette cases by portly well fed gentlemen in formal wear, themselves puffing on expensive Havana cigars.'

'The Restaurant, running the whole width of the ship, is veneered with bleached London plane tree burr, finished in a delicate coffee-and-milk colouring, as a background for evening frocks.'

Queen Elizabeth Cabin Class supplement, 1946

The new Queens still retain the custom of dressing for dinner. The wife of one wealthy businessman regularly booked two suites on the QE2 in the late 1970s, one for herself and her husband and one for her clothes. Her personal New York designer ran up several outfits for each day of a 90 day world cruise. 'I can't stand to wear the same thing twice. I want to come out every day looking as beautiful as your gorgeous ship.'

'The one essential garment for a man aboard a ship is a dinner jacket. He can dispense with all else, but the dinner jacket is as necessary to an ocean traveller as a tailcoat is to a waiter. Without it you may not, except on the first and last nights out, come down to dinner. Without it you will have to sneak out of the smoking-room at eight pm. Without it you will have no dances and no Great Moments with the young thing in crepe marocain on the lee of the starboard ventilator.'

Basil Woon, *the Frantic Atlantic,* 1927

R.M.S. "Campania."   Friday, September 3, 1909.

Menu.

Pea Soup.

Haddock, Anchovy Sauce.

Macaroni a l'Italienne.

Roast Turkey, Sauce Espagnole.

Ox Tongue, Spinach.

Roast Rib of Beef, Horseradish.

———

Boiled Potatoes.

Portugal Onions.   Boiled Rice.

———

Bread and Butter Pudding.

Apple Tart.   Lemon Jelly.

Fancy Pastry.

———

Ice Cream.   Dessert.

Cheese.   Coffee.

'I'D LIKE'
Menus Through Time

'I will have a dozen natives, some borscht Polonaise, a roast partridge with orange salad. Then bring me a savoury of mushrooms stewed with bay leaves and served on a wisp of Wiltshire bacon.' First class passenger, *Aquitania*, 1925

Above, left A beautifully illustrated menu cover from the Batavia in 1882.
Above, middle Golden Jubilee celebration menu, 1890.
Above, right 1978 and real paper streamers suggested the smoking funnel on this novelty menu cover from the QE2.

SPOTTING THE SHIPPING LINE

Funnels and house flags

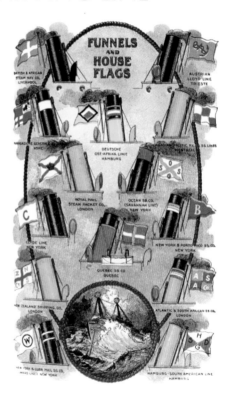

Left and below Passengers on the Laconia II (1921) could identify what ship was coming over the horizon in 'My Trip Abroad', their personal log book.

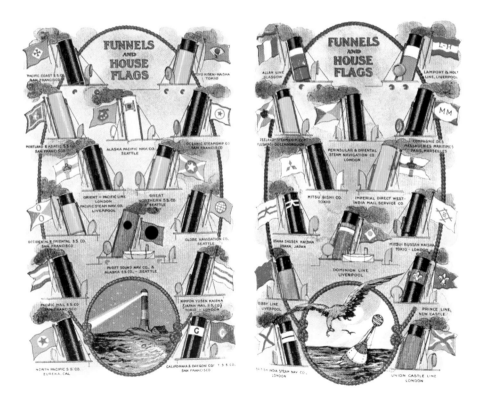

ROCK LIGHT TO ROBBINS REEF

Lighthouses en route

Passengers crossing from Liverpool searched the night skies for the first white flashes and red lights that signalled their approach to New York.

Above Thatchers Island, Cape Ann, Massachusetts.
Right Route map from Second Cabin Passenger List, Campania, 1st September, 1909.

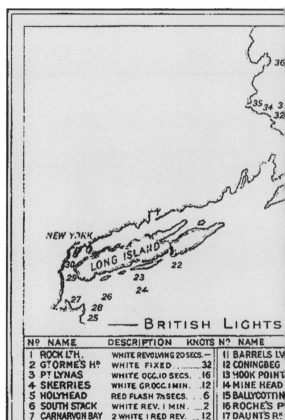

AMERICAN

— BRITISH LIGHTS

Nº	NAME	DESCRIPTION	KNOTS	Nº	NAME
1	ROCK LᵀH.	WHITE REVOLVING 20 SECS. —		11	BARRELS LV
2	GᵀORME'S Hᴰ	WHITE FIXED	32	12	CONINGBEG
3	PᵀLYNAS	WHITE OCC.10 SECS.	16	13	HOOK POINT
4	SKERRIES	WHITE GP.OCC.1 MIN.	12	14	MINE HEAD
5	HOLYHEAD	RED FLASH 7½ SECS.	6	15	BALLYCOTTIN
6	SOUTH STACK	WHITE REV. 1 MIN.	2	16	ROCHE'S Pᵀ
7	CARNARVON BAY	2 WHITE 1 RED REV.	12	17	DAUNT'S Rᴷ
8	BARDSEY Iᴰ.	WHITE OCC. 30 SECS.	16	18	OLD HᴰKINSA
9	SᵀMARKLOW	WHITE REV. 30 SECS.	28	19	GALLEY HEA
10	TUSKAR Rᴷ	WHITE & RED REV.1MIN.	30	20	FASTNET

THE FIGURES ON RIGHT HAN...

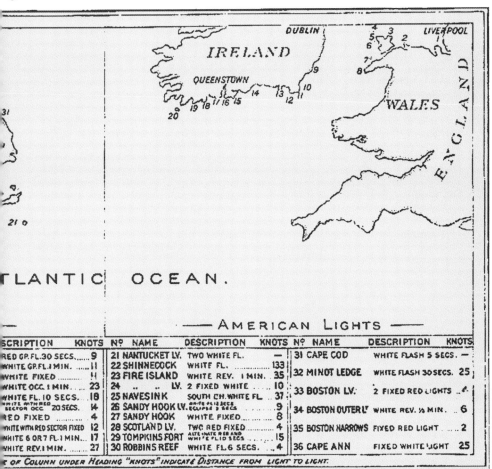

IRELAND

DUBLIN · LIVERPOOL

QUEENSTOWN

WALES

ENGLAND

ATLANTIC OCEAN.

— AMERICAN LIGHTS —

Nº NAME	DESCRIPTION	KNOTS	Nº NAME	DESCRIPTION	KNOTS	Nº NAME	DESCRIPTION	KNOTS
	RED GP. FL. 30 SECS.	9	21 NANTUCKET LV.	TWO WHITE FL.	—	31 CAPE COD	WHITE FLASH 5 SECS.	—
	WHITE GP. FL. 1 MIN.	11	22 SHINNECOCK	WHITE FL.	133	32 MINOT LEDGE	WHITE FLASH 30 SECS.	25
	WHITE FIXED	11	23 FIRE ISLAND	WHITE REV. 1 MIN.	35	33 BOSTON LV.	2 FIXED RED LIGHTS	4
	WHITE OCC. 1 MIN.	23	24 " " LV.	2 FIXED WHITE	10			
	WHITE FL. 10 SECS.	18	25 NAVESINK	SOUTH CH. WHITE FL.	37	34 BOSTON OUTER LT	WHITE REV. ½ MIN.	6
	WHITE WITH RED SECTOR OCC. 20 SECS.	14	26 SANDY HOOK LV.	WHITE FL. 3 SECS.	9			
	RED FIXED	4	27 SANDY HOOK	WHITE FIXED	8	35 BOSTON NARROWS	FIXED RED LIGHT	2
	WHITE WITH RED SECTOR FIXED	12	28 SCOTLAND LV.	TWO RED FIXED	4			
	WHITE 6 OR 7 FL. 1 MIN.	17	29 TOMPKINS FORT	ALTERNATE RED AND WHITE FL. 10 SECS.	15	36 CAPE ANN	FIXED WHITE LIGHT	25
	WHITE REV. 1 MIN.	27	30 ROBBINS REEF	WHITE FL. 6 SECS.	4			

...E OF COLUMN UNDER HEADING "KNOTS" INDICATE DISTANCE FROM LIGHT TO LIGHT.

THE CUNARD PASSENGER FLEET
1840-2005

Name	Gross tonnage	Cunard owned from	to	Name	Gross tonnage	Cunard owned from	to
Abyssinia	3,376	1870	1880	Aurania	7,269	1883	1905
Acadia	1,154	1840	1848	Aurania II	13,936	1917	1918
Africa	2,226	1850	1868	Aurania III	13,984	1924	1942
Alaunia	13,405	1913	1916	Ausonia	7,907	1911	1918
Alaunia II	14,040	1925	1944	Ausonia II	13,912	1922	1944
Albania	7,640	1911	1912	Australasian	2,902	1860	1876
Albania II	12,768	1921	1930	Balbec	774	1853	1884
Aleppo	2,056	1865	1909	Batavia	2,553	1870	1887
Algeria	3,428	1870	1882	Berengaria	52,226	1919	1938
Alps	1,440	1852	1859	Bothnia	4,535	1874	1896
America	1,826	1848	1866	Britannia	1,135	1840	1848
Andania	13,405	1913	1918	Britannic III	26,943	1935	1960
Andania II	13,950	1922	1940	British Queen	772	1851	1899
Andes	1,440	1852	1859	Caledonia	1,138	1840	1850
Antonia	13,867	1922	1942	California	8,662	1907	1917
Aquitania	45,647	1914	1949	Cambria	1,423	1844	1860
Arabia	2,402	1853	1864	Cameronia	10,963	1915	1917
Ascania	9,111	1911	1918	Cameronia II	16,280	1921	1935
Ascania II	14,013	1925	1956	Campania	12,950	1893	1918
Asia	2,226	1850	1867	Canada	1,831	1848	1867
Athenia	13,465	1923	1935	Carinthia II	20,277	1925	1940
Atlas	2,393	1860	1896	Carinthia III	21,947	1956	1968

Name	Gross tonnage	Cunard owned from	to	Name	Gross tonnage	Cunard owned from	to
Carmania	19,524	1905	1931	Franconia	18,150	1911	1916
Caronia	19,687	1905	1933	Franconia II	20,158	1923	1956
Caronia II	34,183	1949	1967	Gallia	4,809	1879	1897
Caronia III	24,492	1983	2004	Georgic	27,759	1934	1956
Carpathia	13,555	1903	1918	Hecla	1,785	1860	1881
Cassandra	8,135	1924	1929	Hibernia	1,422	1843	1850
Catalonia	4,481	1881	1901	Homeric	34,352	1935	1936
Cephalonia	5,517	1882	1901	Ivernia	14,058	1900	1916
China	2,638	1862	1880	Ivernia II	17,707	1955	1973
Columbia	1,175	1841	1843	Java	2,696	1865	1878
Crown Dynasty	19,089	1994	1997	Jura	2,241	1857	1861
Crown Jewel	19,089	1993	1995	Karnak	1,116	1855	1862
Crown Monarch	19,089	1993	1994	Kedar	1,863	1860	1897
Cuba	2,668	1864	1876	Laconia	18,099	1912	1917
Cunard Adventurer	14,110	1971	1977	Laconia II	19,860	1921	1942
Cunard Ambassador	14,151	1972	1974	Lancastria	16,243	1922	1940
Cunard Countess	7,495	1976	1996	Laurentic	18,724	1934	1940
Cunard Princess	17,495	1977	1995	Lebanon	1,373	1855	1859
Czar	6,503	1917	1921	Letitia	13,475	1925	1960
Damascus	1,213	1856	1861	Lucania	12,952	1893	1909
Emeu	1,358	1854	1857	Lusitania	31,550	1907	1915
Etna	2,215	1855	1881	Majestic	56,551	1934	1939
Etruria	7,718	1885	1910	Malta	2,132	1866	1889
Europa	1,834	1848	1867	Marathon	1,784	1861	1889
Feltria	5,254	1916	1917	Mauretania	31,938	1907	1935
Flavia	9,285	1916	1918	Mauretania II	35,738	1939	1965

Name	Gross tonnage	Cunard owned from	to
Media	13,345	1947	1961
Melita	1,254	1853	1868
Nemesis	2,717	1869	1869
Niagara	1,824	1848	1866
Olympic	45,342	1934	1935
Olympus	1,794	1860	1881
Orduna	15,499	1914	1920
Oregon	7,324	1884	1886
Palestine	1,800	1860	1872
Palmyra	2,044	1866	1896
Pannonia	9,851	1904	1922
Parthia	3,167	1870	1883
Parthia II	13,362	1948	1963
Pavonia	5,588	1882	1900
Persia	3,300	1856	1872
Prinses Irene	8,533	1964	1965
Queen Elizabeth	83,673	1940	1968
Queen Elizabeth 2	70,327	1969	-
Queen Mary	80,774	1936	1967
Queen Mary 2	150,000	2004	-
Royal George	11,146	1919	1922
Royal Viking Sun	37,845	1994	1999
Russia	2,960	1867	1880
Sagafjord	20,147	1983	1997
Samaria	2,574	1869	1896
Samaria II	19,602	1922	1955

Name	Gross tonnage	Cunard owned from	to
Saragossa	2,263	1874	1880
Saxonia	14,281	1900	1925
Saxonia II	21,637	1954	1969
Scotia	3,817	1862	1879
Scythia	4,557	1875	1898
Scythia II	19,730	1921	1958
Sea Goddess	4,253	1986	1999
Sea Goddess II	4,253	1986	1999
Servia	7,392	1881	1902
Siberia	2,498	1867	1880
Sidon	1,872	1863	1885
Slavonia	10,606	1904	1909
Sylvania	5,598	1895	1910
Sylvania II	21,989	1957	1968
Tarifa	2,058	1865	1898
Taurus	1,126	1853	1859
Teneriffe	1,127	1854	1859
Transylvania	14,315	1914	1917
Tripoli	2,057	1865	1872
Tuscania	14,348	1915	1918
Tuscania II	16,991	1926	1939
Ultonia	8,845	1898	1917
Umbria	7,718	1884	1910
Vauban	10,660	1919	1922

Right Oops! Even spelling 'Queen' can pose problems much less Mauretania. Queen Mary 2, 2005.

HALF THE FUN
The daily programme on board

Every morning passengers in each class woke to find the daily programme of events had been slipped under the cabin door. Here is how passengers on the Queen Mary might fill in their day in 1956.

R.M.S. "QUEEN MARY"   Saturday, September 1, 1956

PROGRAMME OF EVENTS

a.m.

7.00—7.00 p.m.—Swimming Pool and Gymnasium open for Exercise (weather and other circumstances permitting)

Passenger List Competition

9.15—Keep-Fit Class (Gentlemen)   Gymnasium

10.00—Movie: Cinema, Prom. Deck
"THE PROUD AND THE PROFANE"
William Holden, Deborah Kerr

10.45—Meeting of Rotarians   First Class Drawing Room

11.00—Keep-Fit Class (Ladies)   Gymnasium

11.15—"Tote" on Daily Run (closes at 11.50 a.m.)   Smoke Room

11.30—Selections at the Hammond Organ   Main Lounge
by Charles Handel—relayed

p.m.

2.00—Movie: Cinema
"THE PROUD AND THE PROFANE"
William Holden, Deborah Kerr

2.15—Recorded Music   Main Lounge
Symphony No. 6 in B Minor, Opus 74, "Pathetique" (Tchaikovsky)
The Philharmonia Orchestra. Conductor: Guido Cantelli

2.30—Meeting of Lions International and Kiwanis
First Class Drawing Room

2.30—Table Tennis Tournament commences   Main Deck

3.45—Music for Tea Time   Main Lounge
Queen Mary String Orchestra, directed by Raoul Bacot

4.00—Children's Tea Party   First Class Restaurant

6.15—News Broadcast (British)   Main Lounge

6.30—News Broadcast (American)   Main Lounge

6.30—Cocktail Music   Mermaid Bar, Prom. Deck
Queen Mary Dance Orchestra, directed by Duggie Campbell

7.45—Orchestral Selections   Main Lounge
Queen Mary String Orchestra, directed by Raoul Bacot

9.15—HORSE RACES   Main Lounge
followed by DANCING
Queen Mary Dance Orchestra, directed by Duggie Campbell
DANCING will continue at approximately 12.30 a.m. in the Rose Room, "A" Deck Aft, after completion in the Main Lounge
Queen Mary Dance Orchestra, directed by Duggie Campbell

CUNARD A-Z
The passenger A list

Eddie **Arcaro**	*1916-1997*	Top US jockey
Cecil **Beaton**	*1904-1980*	Photographer to the rich and famous
Charles **Chaplin**	*1889-1977*	The Everyman of film
Marlene **Dietrich**	*1901-1992*	Sultry on-screen vamp and cabaret singer
Duke **Ellington**	*1899-1974*	Maestro of jazz
Douglas **Fairbanks Jnr**	*1909-2000*	Romantic hero on and off screen
Clark **Gable**	*1901-1960*	The heart breaker in 'Gone with the Wind'
Rita **Hayworth**	*1918-1985*	Hollywood's greatest pin-up girl
Shah of **Iran**	*1919-1980*	Western playboy and eastern ruler
Glynis **Johns**	*1923-*	Beautiful, husky-voiced, British actress
Buster **Keaton**	*1895-1966*	The greatest comic of the silent screen
Stan **Laurel**	*1890-1965*	Comic foil to 'fat man' Oliver Hardy
Somerset **Maugham**	*1874-1965*	Master of the short story
David **Niven**	*1910-1983*	The seriously handsome leading man
Jackie **Onassis**	*1929-1994*	The talented widow of President Kennedy
Gregory **Peck**	*1919-2003*	The decent upright citizen on and off screen
Queen Elizabeth	*1900-2002*	Wife of King George VI and later 'Queen Mum'
Ginger **Rogers**	*1911-1995*	Partner to Fred Astaire - 'Shall We Dance?'
Barbara **Stanwyck**	*1907-1990*	Hollywood's femme fatale
Sophie **Tucker**	*1884-1966*	One of the world's greatest live entertainers
Edward **Underdown**	*1908-1989*	British jockey and 1950s film star
Andrei **Vyshinsky**	*1883-1954*	Soviet Foreign Minister
Johnny **Weismuller**	*1904-1984*	Star of Tarzan and Jungle Jim films
X	*1840-*	The celebs who travelled incognito
Loretta **Young**	*1913-2000*	'Naughty but nice' film actress
Ziegfeld Girl	*1905-?*	Alias film star Myrna Loy

OVER HERE

Bringing over US troops 1942-45

The Queens and other Cunarders ferried hundreds of thousands of GIs to Europe. Standing Orders for American Troops gave the following warning. 'The ship will be very crowded … Officers and Men should not view this trip as a vacation: it will be anything but that.'

It was indeed far from a vacation. Many soldiers had never seen the sea before, much less travelled through the war zone of the Atlantic in a winter storm with U-boats lurking below and enemy bombers above. Fear was ever present. On one occasion, with 15,000 troops on board, the Queen Mary rolled within two degrees of the point of no return after she encountered a freak 75 ft high wall of water in mid-Atlantic.

Every space on the liners was put to use. Troops slept in standee bunks up to seven high: vertigo could be as much a problem as seasickness. A cabin class, two person stateroom accommodated 21 men sleeping barely 18 inches apart. The worst billets were the indoor swimming pools which were turned into dormitories. Troops sometimes slept in shifts in the same bunk or made do with a rug on the floor.

Although the kitchens operated round the clock, sheer numbers meant that troops were rationed to two meals a day, each with six sittings. Eight and a half tons of potatoes, 31,000 eggs and three quarters of a ton of sausages were consumed daily on the Queen Elizabeth during a typical Atlantic run. Eggs were boiled in garbage bins filled by steam hoses.

Life was highly regulated – no waving a last farewell to New York, no lights on deck, no smoking on the upper decks at night. No rubbish to be thrown overboard, no moving to other sections of the ship, no hard drinking and certainly no sex. When service women were on board, segregation sentries were posted to ensure that the GIs kept to their quarters. The problem of getting troops to carry their life jackets was finally solved by a sentry confiscating the offender's left shoe until he returned to his bunk for his jacket. The sale of gum in the canteens was eventually banned because so much was stuck to the decks.

The GIs remember their crossings.

'We trucked up the pier and were conducted into this building. We knew it wasn't really a building but that was the size of the ship.'

'I had seventeen dollars in my pocket before I got involved in a black jack game, and by the time I realized we were passing the Statue of Liberty leaving the States, I was already flat broke.'

'On the deck below us were WACs (Women's Army Corps) and nurses. Guys were sending notes to the women, tying them on a piece of string and lowering the string down. But instead of female nurses or WACs there were MPs (Military Police) down there, and they were the ones answering the notes!'

'We had bunk-type beds. As the ship made a violent turn in its zig-zag motion it tilted and we were thrown against the bulkhead. A few minutes later, as it turned in the other direction, we had to struggle to keep from being thrown over the edge of the bed and on to the deck. This went on all night long.'

'The bedding arrangements were absolutely unbelievable. They had steel poles that went from ceiling to deck and attached to these, between each pair of poles, were bunks that would fold up each day so you could walk by. They had as many as six bunks and you only had a maximum of two feet between each bunk for sleeping. When a GI gets in the bunk, he sags down at least six inches so you only had about 18 inches.'

'We were placed on alert. We were instructed to stand on the outside deck with our life belts on. They told us - this is standard practice going into a harbour where the subs could be lying in wait.'

'On 6th July the Queen docked for the night in Glasgow. It was late afternoon, and lots of small boats gathered around the Elizabeth with people on board calling for American cigarettes. We threw them over the sides and children dived in after them.'

The GIs left their mark on the liners. When the Queen Mary was finally demobbed in 1946 millions of graffiti had to be removed from her deck rails.

ANIMALS ON BOARD
Wanted or not wanted on voyage

From circus elephants to pampered pooches, animals have always travelled Cunard.

On her maiden voyage in 1840, the Britannia had three cats on board. Passengers were forbidden to feed them in case they lost their appetite for rats. Rats were 'not wanted on voyage' even on 20th century liners. There was a plague of rats on the Berengaria on an early 1920s crossing after their lairs were flooded in a storm.

Some pets were stars in their own right. Mr Ramshaw, a 22 year old eagle, made at least 21 crossings on mid 20th century liners: his owner claimed that his bird was the only trained golden eagle in the world. Mr Ramshaw was accommodated near the butcher's shop which supplied him with chicken heads. Rin-Tin-Tin, the star of 36 silent films, travelled on the Berengaria. Although his keeper had a first class ticket, he chose to remain 24 hours a day with the dog on the tourist class deck. Tom Mix and Tony, the stars of the 'Miracle Rider' series, regularly rode up the first class gangway. Tony, a seasoned traveller, was fitted with special rubber shoes to stop him slipping about the decks.

In 1928 Cunard granted Buddy, the first guide dog to be trained by Frank Morris, the founder of The Seeing Eye, a free passage on the Tuscania II. After cashing a traveller's check in the purser's office, Morris lay down on his bunk for a nap. He woke when Buddy dropped his wallet on his chest. Buddy had carried it half the length of the ship from the purser's office.

Animals were even part of the décor on the Berengaria. In the mid 1930s canaries in cages hung from the balconies of the restaurant, special springs keeping the cages upright even when the ship rolled. One of the bellboys' duties was to feed them.

There were 26 kennels in two tiers on the Queen Mary, each with a removable teak floor, skylight, hot and cold running water and central heating. On one visit to the ship the dog-loving Duke of Windsor remarked that it was a shame that there was no lamp post beside the kennels. Cunard immediately obeyed the royal command, later remembering to install a lamp post convenience on the QE2.

Cunard offered a dog walking service. One bellboy on the Queen Mary recalled: 'We used to get some terrible little dogs - always fighting each other. And you'd have to drag them around the deck for about half an hour and take them to see their owners on the prom deck.'

Homing pigeons and migrating birds are occasionally blown off course. In 2001 a racing pigeon landed, exhausted, on the bridge of the QE2 in mid-Atlantic. Given a perch in the kennels and fed a special menu of corn, the bird became a great favourite with passengers who christened it 'Coo E 2'. QM2's first stowaway was a teenage tern which landed on the balcony of a suite, 485 miles due east of Cape Race at the end of April, 2004. The bird was rushed to the medical centre where it was fed smoked salmon and caviar before being released as the ship neared the UK.

The crew were known to smuggle exotic animals on board as pets. A linotype operator

Above A pony travelled on the Queen Mary in the late Thirties.

on the Queen Elizabeth kept a monkey in a bread cage in the Print Shop. When let out for a breather, the monkey leaped straight into the air conditioning shaft in the ceiling. It hid there for four days until the ship reached Southampton when it was bribed out with a large bowl of fruit. During a 1980 QE2 cruise to South America, a crew member smuggled aboard Basil the pet boa constrictor along with a large live white rat for his Sunday lunch. Off the coast of Venezuela, Basil, with the rat in his mouth, made a break for freedom. The culprits were eventually cornered and cast overboard: they were last seen swimming for the shore.

THE BLUE RIBAND
Cunard speed record breakers

Although the shipping line officially disapproved of racing, individual captains liked to put their thoroughbreds through their paces. Cunarders broke the record fifty times.

Westbound crossing

Date	Vessel	Days:hrs:min	Knots
1841	Columbia	10:19:00	9.78
1845	Cambria	09:20:30	10.71
1848	America	09:00:16	11.71
1848	Europa	08:23:00	11.79
1850	Asia	08:14:50	12.25
1856	Persia	09:16:16	13.11
1863	Scotia	08:03:00	14.46
1885	Etruria	06:05:31	18.73
1887	Umbria	06:04:12	19.22
1888	Etruria	06:01:55	19.56
1893	Campania	05:15:37	21.12
1894	Campania	05:09:29	21.44
1894	Lucania	05:08:38	21.65
1894	Lucania	05:07:48	21.75
1894	Lucania	05:07:23	21.81
1907	Lusitania	04:19:52	23.99
1908	Lusitania	04:20:22	24.83
1908	Lusitania	04:19:36	25.01
1909	Lusitania	04:16:40	25.65
1909	Mauretania	04:10:51	26.06
1936	Queen Mary	04:00:27	30.14
1938	Queen Mary	03:21:48	30.99

Note: The record was calculated on the average speed, the crossing time depending on the route taken.

Left Queen Mary entering New York.

Eastbound crossing

Date	Vessel	Days:hrs:min	Knots
1840	Britannia	09:21:44	10.98
1843	Columbia	09:12:00	11.11
1843	Hibernia	09:10:44	11.18
1843	Hibernia	08:22:44	11.80
1849	Canada	08:12:44	12.38
1856	Persia	09:10:22	13.46
1856	Persia	09:03:24	13.89
1856	Persia	08:23:19	14.15
1863	Scotia	08:05:42	14.16
1884	Oregon	06:12:54	18.18
1884	Oregon	06:11:09	18.39
1885	Etruria	06:09:00	18.44
1888	Etruria	06:04:50	19.36
1893	Campania	05:17:27	21.30
1894	Lucania	03:13:28	21.81
1894	Lucania	05:12:59	21.90
1895	Lucania	05:11:40	22.00
1907	Lusitania	04:22:53	23.61
1907	Mauretania	04:22:33	23.69
1908	Mauretania	05:02:41	23.90
1908	Mauretania	05:00:05	24.42
1909	Mauretania	04:20:27	25.16
1909	Mauretania	04:18:35	25.61
1909	Mauretania	04:18:11	25.70
1909	Mauretania	04:17:21	25.88
1924	Mauretania	05:01:49	26.25
1936	Queen Mary	03:23:57	30.63
1938	Queen Mary	03:20:42	31.69

FLOATING PALACES
Reviews of Cunard interiors

From the late 19th century Cunard's publicity department, the press and travellers themselves used every superlative in the dictionary to describe the interiors of the liners. There were few dissenting voices.

'Its general style is Italian … somewhat sobered down by an air of British substantiality.'

Contemporary review of the Campania (1893)

'The ladies saloon is a charming retreat, the carpets are of a very pretty pattern, the lounges are wide, the cushions impart a sense of buoyancy, geraniums are blooming and the mignonette is exhaling its sweetness. It is a club house and boudoir combined.'

Contemporary review of the Campania (1893)

'The stately chambers of a palace rather than accommodation within the steel walls of a ship'

Cunard publicity for the Lucania (1893)

'It was a beautiful thing all-told: its long cherry-wood panelled halls, its heavy porcelain baths, its dainty state rooms fitted with lamps, bureaus, writing desks, wash stands, closets and the like.'

US author **Theodore Dreiser** travelling on the Mauretania (1907)

'Regal suites consisting of two bedrooms, a private dining room and butler's pantry, reception room and bathroom are adorned with delicate tapestries; furnished with Sheraton dressing tables, brocaded settees, bedsteads of brass and fitted with the best of bedding, blankets and linen, the whole cared for by skilled fingers.'

1908 Cunard brochure for the Lusitania

'*A wonderful impression of quiet grandeur ... a room unequalled in any steamship and rarely surpassed even in a palace.*'

'*The Engineer*', 1907 of the Mauretania's Grand Saloon

Left Dining room on the Lusitania (1907).

'The Aquitania is not a floating hotel any more than a good yacht is a floating flat. Hotels and flats are full of noise and restlessness and are generally overcrowded. The Wonder Ship is a glorious country house with just the right number of people in it and plenty of room for them all.'

1920s Cunard brochure 'RMS Aquitania'

'She was a ship of gloomy panelled majesty, hard to handle, clumsy and Teutonic, a creation of industry without pretensions to beauty ... a bejewelled ferryboat for the rich and titled.'

Captain Grattidge of the German designed Berengaria (1919)

'She is probably the prettiest chunk of steamship they've ever allowed to splash down the ways of a shipyard.'

US journalist reporting on the Carinthia II (1925)

'Here is revealed indeed the essential destiny of the Queen Mary to be lived in luxuriously but with good taste, in settings of exceptional splendour but without exaggeration ... Spacious almost beyond belief her hospitality is yet warm and intimate.'

'Queen Mary Cabin Class Deck Plan', 1936

Above Left Accommodation brochure, Aquitania.
Above Brochure celebrating the opulence of the Aquitania, 1914.

'*The keynote is solid comfort and snugness, characteristic of the best type of London or New York club, where deep leather armchairs in alcoves invite intimate conversations and a real coal fire blazes cheerfully in the grate.*'

'*Daily Telegraph*', 1936 of the Queen Mary's Smoking Room

'*The pool itself is lined with golden quartzite, a stone used in the days of the Pharoahs. Seen through the seawater, it gives the impression of a sandy pool.*'

'*Queen Elizabeth Accommodation Plan*' c1950

'*She's a swinging super-ship, controversially beautiful. She has a regal beauty all of her own. It's there for all to see, built into her smooth and simple, sleek and graceful lines. A ship surely to stir the hearts of a maritime nation.*'

'*Daily Mirror*', 1968 of the QE2

'*There's nothing of the old Lady about the new Queen Elizabeth Two. She is smart, crisp and modern.*'

'*Daily Telegraph*', 1968

'*Mild but expensive vulgarity*'

Review of the Queen Mary in '*Architect and Building News*', 1936

Above First class dining room, Queen Mary.

THE PIG 'N' WHISTLE

How crew spent their leisure

On 20th century liners crew social life centred on the Pig and Whistle off the High Street, the ship's main working alleyway. Regardless of the individual ship, the pub was always called the Pig, possibly taking its name from the Pig and Whistle in Liverpool. a popular haunt on the night before sailing day.

For many crew on the Queen Mary going for a pint at the Pig involved a quarter of a mile walk from their cabin. The Sergeant-at-Arms, the ship's policeman, often posted a 'bouncer' near the door. Beside it there was an area for playing darts which doubled up as a baggage handling area when in port. The inside of the Pig was a world away from the glamour of passenger bars. Its walls were steel bulkheads and it was decked with teak planking. Fittings included exposed light bulbs and hand-me-down tables and chairs.

The Pig 'n' Whistle was male only, stewardesses being expected to amuse themselves and their female colleagues in their cabins. It was also largely out of bounds for bellboys.

Crew members recall the Pig:

'Our cabin was right up at the forward end just before the Pig and Whistle. We could go up there for lemonades and packets of crisps but no matter how hard we tried, as bellboys, we couldn't get any booze.'

'On the Berengaria in the 1930s housey-housey was popular in the Pig 'n' Whistle. The game was introduced by a short Liverpool cook, inevitably called Scouse. His language was choice and his accent thick. If they could not catch the number, players would shout out: 'What was the last number Scouse?' His reply would turn the air blue and send the game into chaos.'

Stewards in the 1930s worked a 12 hour day or more. 'We had to get up at 6.30 am and do a 'scrub out' - scrubbing part of a deck or polishing brasses in the toilets. We had to be standing at table for breakfast at 8am until 9.30am. At 11 o'clock we had to go round the decks with hot drinks for the passengers. Then we had to attend our tables for lunch from 12.30 to 1.30. Then we had to go around the decks again for afternoon teas at 4pm. Then dinner from 6.30 to 7.30. After that we went to the Pig and Whistle from about 9pm till 10.30.'

'The chief of the print room was a great admirer of the lager which could be obtained from the Pig and Whistle. My mission was to obtain the lager for the chief which would cement our working relationship for the voyage to NY. This involved ordering ten pints from the barman and carrying five pints in each hand from the bar at the rear, walking half the length of the ship, descending two flights of stairs and entering the print shop without spilling a drop. This was accomplished with flying colours.'

'You could bet on almost anything in the Queen Mary's Pig 'n' Whistle.'

Other entertainments included a pool on the miles covered by the liner on the previous day, boxing tournaments and darts competitions. Crew would also sneak into passenger cinemas once the lights were down. 'One of the great treats for us bellboys was to sit behind the screen of the Queen Mary's first class cinema, and although we had to watch the film in reverse we thought it was tremendous.' Some crew also pursued hobbies from carving souvenirs to sell to passengers to making ship models.

BUMPS AND SCRAPES
Early collisions and groundings

Despite Samuel Cunard's watchword of 'Safety First', collisions and groundings were inevitable, given the fogs, ice and storms of the North Atlantic and the lack of navigation aids.

Cunard's first serious accident was not long in coming. In July, 1843 Samuel was in Halifax awaiting the arrival of the Columbia (1840), sailing up from Boston with 85 passengers, cargo and the mail. Nearly two days later, the Acadia (1840) came into port with the news that the Columbia had been carried off course in fog and had run aground on the Devil's Rib reef outside Halifax. Samuel sailed anxiously to the rescue. By the time he arrived, the crew, with the aid of the light keeper, had helped all the passengers ashore and salvaged the mail. Three schooner-loads of cargo and equipment were also rescued before the Columbia broke up in a storm.

A year later the Britannia (1840) became trapped by ice in Boston Harbor. The city's merchants organised a team of lumberjacks and labourers to plough a seven mile channel through the ice to the open sea. Half the population of Boston skated alongside as the Britannia slowly made her way through the channel. Concerned that Cunard might desert Boston for New York, the merchants waived the bill.

The Europa (1848) was an accident-prone vessel. In 1849 she collided in dense fog with the US emigrant ship, Charles Bartlett, which sank with the loss of 135 lives. The Europa's passengers formed a committee to investigate which concluded: 'Everything was done by the commander, the officers, and the crew of the Europa to prevent the lamentable disaster, and everything tried after its occurrence to save lives and to minister to the comforts of the survivors.' Nine years later the Europa hit fellow Cunarder, the Arabia (1853) off Newfoundland: despite both being badly damaged they managed to limp into port.

In 1856 Cunard launched the Persia, the largest ship on the North Atlantic. At the time it faced serious competition for supremacy of the Atlantic from the American Collins Line. Charles McIver commented that Collins was 'pretty much in the situation of finding that breaking our windows with sovereigns, tho' very fine fun, is too costly to keep up.' He was right: Edward Collins over-reached himself by putting speed before safety and several of his ships foundered. The final straw was the loss of the Pacific which vanished in mid-Atlantic with over 180 passengers while racing Cunard's Persia for the speed record. Although the Persia collided with an iceberg, she managed to limp into New York under sail, expecting to be greeted by the Pacific's gloating crew.

On 14th March, 1886 off Long Island, the Oregon which Cunard had recently bought from the bankrupt Guion Line, was rammed on the port side just ahead of the bridge by a low sailing vessel. This was believed to be the Charles H. Morse, a three masted coasting schooner out of Maine laden with coal. The blow left two holes in the Oregon's side: the Morse was never seen again. The Oregon's 896 passengers and crew took to the lifeboats in an orderly manner and although the ship sank shortly thereafter no lives were lost.

On 10th November, 1888, the Umbria collided with the cargo vessel Iberia in dense fog, as she sailed out of New York Harbor. Despite both ships taking avoiding action, the Umbria was unable to stop and sliced a 14 ft section off the stern of the smaller vessel. Although passengers on the badly damaged Umbria barely felt a jolt, the Iberia sank, fortunately not before the Umbria managed to rescue her crew.

Despite collisions and groundings, Cunard managed to maintain its record of not losing a passenger at sea into the 20th century. In 1905 a rogue wave hit the Campania in mid-Atlantic and swept five steerage passengers into the sea.

Below Persia (1856).

ROYAL SEND-OFF

Royal launches, visits and crossings

Royals who have launched, visited or travelled on Cunard liners include:

1861 *Prince Alfred* Passenger on the Arabia

1920s *Sultan of Jahore* Passenger on the Berengaria

1920s *Princess Xenia Georgevna of Russia* Passenger on the Aquitania

1920 *Queen Marie of Romania* Passenger on the Berengaria

1924 *Future Edward VIII* Passenger on the Berengaria

1934 *George V and Queen Mary* Launched Queen Mary

1936 *Princess Elizabeth* Visited the Queen Mary before her maiden voyage

1938 *Queen Elizabeth* Launched Queen Elizabeth

1946 *Queen Elizabeth* Visited Queen Elizabeth

1947 *Princess Elizabeth* Launched Caronia II

1948 *Duke of Edinburgh* Joined Caronia II on her sea trials

1950s *Shah of Persia and Empress Soraya* Passengers, Queen Mary

1950s *Ex-King Peter of Yugoslavia* Passenger on the Queen Mary

1950s *The Duke and Duchess of Windsor* Passengers on the Queen Mary

1950s *Crown Prince Akihito of Japan* Passenger on the Queen Mary and QE2

1952 *Future King Faisal II of Iraq* Passenger on the Queen Mary

1952 *King Hussein of Jordan* Passenger on the Queen Mary and QE2

1954 *Queen Mother* Passenger on the Queen Elizabeth and Queen Mary

1967 *Queen Elizabeth* Launched QE2

1968 *Queen Mother* Visited Queen Elizabeth after her last voyage

1969 *Queen Elizabeth* Visited QE2 before her maiden voyage

1969 *Prince Charles* Joined QE2 on her sea trials

1977 *Princess Grace of Monaco* Christened the Cunard Princess

Left to right Queen Elizabeth and Princess
Elizabeth visiting the Queen Elizabeth,
1948: the Queen visiting the QE2, 1990:
Princess Diana on the QE2, 1986.

1977   *Queen Elizabeth* Watched QE2 preparing for Jubilee Review
1982   *Queen Mother* Welcomed QE2 home after Falklands War
1986   *Queen Mother* Visited QE2 on 50th anniversary of Queen Mary
1986   *Diana Princess of Wales* Visited QE2 after her major refit
1988   *Queen Mother* Visited QE2 on 50th anniversary of Queen Elizabeth
1990   *Queen Elizabeth* Boarded QE2 as part of Spithead Review
1992   *Duke of Edinburgh/Prince Edward* Attended overnight charity gala on QE2
1993   *Prince Edward* Visited QE2 as part of Queen's 40th Anniversary celebrations
2004   *Queen Elizabeth* Named Queen Mary 2

Many more have travelled on Cunard liners from Queen Victoria's sons on visits to Canada
to the Sultan of Brunei.

AYE AYE, SIR

Ranks and epaulettes

DECK

6 Gold
Master

4 Gold
Staff Captain

3.5 Gold
Chief Officer

3 Gold
Principal Medical Officer, Safety
Officer, Environmental Officer,
Medical Officer

2.5 Gold
First Officer

2.5 Gold w/S
Security Officer

2 Gold
Second Officer, Nursing Sister

1.5 Gold
Third Officer

'The Cunard people would not take
Noah himself as First Mate till they
had worked him up through the all
the lower grades and tried him ten
years or such matter.'

Mark Twain

HOTEL

4 Gold w/white
Hotel Manager

3.5 Gold w/white
F & B Manager

3 Gold w/white
Chief Purser, Executive Chef, Cruise Director, Executive Housekeeper

2.5 Gold w/white
Crew Purser, Purser Guest Services, Maitre D', Lido Manager, Public Room Manager, Asst. F & B Manager, Provision Master, Crew Housekeeper, Executive Sous Chef, Chef de Cuisine

2 Gold w/white
Housekeeper, Night Purser, F & B Controller, Cashier, Concierge, Asst. Purser,

1.5 Gold w/white
Asst. Crew Purser, Asst. Provisions Manager, Sanitation Officer

1 Gold w/white
Hotel Manager's Personal Assistant, Sous Chef, Asst. Housekeeper, Asst. Maitre D', Technical Secretary, Captain's Secretary

TECHNICAL

4 Gold w/maroon
Chief Engineer, Staff Chief Engineer

3.5 Gold w/maroon
Ship's Services Manager, Chief Electrical Engineer

3 Gold w/maroon
First Engineer, First Electrical Engineer, First Computer Systems Officer, First Electronics Office

2.5 Gold w/maroon
Refrigeration/HVAC Engineer, Second Engineer, Second Computer Systems Officer, Second Electronics Officer, Accomodation Services Engineer, Second Electrical Engineer

2 Gold w/maroon
Technical Storekeeper, Third Electrical Engineer, Third Engineer

1.5 Gold w/maroon
Fourth Engineer, Hotel Services Engineer

1 Gold w/maroon
Fifth Engineer, Deck Services Engineer

0.5 Gold w/maroon
Uncertified Engineer

Left Commodore Bisset, 1945.

Photographed on board R.M.S. "QUEEN MARY"

STARS ABOARD

How celebrities spent their time at sea

Cunard described the Berengaria in the 1920s as 'Hollywood afloat'. Film stars, comedians, actors, singers and sportsmen all shuttled across the Atlantic. Some took the opportunity to escape briefly from the public eye while others revelled in the attention from star-struck passengers.

During the Queen Mary's sea trials, British Olympic runner Lord Burghley conducted his own speed trials running a lap of 400 yards in evening dress around the Promenade Deck in under 60 seconds.

On one crossing on the Berengaria the tragic-comedian Charlie Chaplin was spotted by Lord Beaverbrook's party, his face hidden and his shoulders apparently shaking with grief. Then he turned round and flashed them a smile - it turned out that he had been shaking a cocktail.

Actor and playwright Noel Coward and Cunard went hand in hand. He was one of the Queens' most frequent travellers

winning over both passengers and crew with his repartee and social graces. He suffered from seasickness even in calm weather and despite his reputation as a bon viveur often ordered bangers and mash.

On one mid-1950s cruise on the Mauretania II, film star Joan Crawford rarely left her suite. She had recently married her fourth and last husband Alfred Steele, Chairman of Pepsi-Cola. She told an officer that her husband was 'a real pain in the you-know-what' and that she had escaped to sort out her problems.

While crossing on the Aquitania in 1921, world heavyweight boxer Jack Dempsey denied his engagement to one of the Dolly Sisters, on the grounds that he could not tell the twin entertainers apart. The Dolly Sisters gave the Aquitania two white Persian cats as a consolation prize. Contrary to his image Dempsey was a quiet and unassuming man, in bed by 10pm and in the gym by 6am.

Right Bob Hope practising his golf swing.

Above Entertainer Jack Buchanan, being photographed photographing.

He neither drank nor smoked and ate a very simple diet. Passengers crowded on deck to watch him practising with his sparring partner in the afternoons.

In the 1950s entertainer Marlene Dietrich was a regular passenger, famous for never being seen at breakfast and rarely for lunch. On making a dramatic entrance at dinner, she followed the advice of her friend, the playwright Sir Noel Coward: 'Always be seen, darling, always be seen'.

In the 1950s Walt Disney and his family spent the evening on the Queen Elizabeth's dance floor, after a meal at the table which they always reserved for its view of the Manhattan skyline in the sunset.

Like his parents, film star and society host Douglas Fairbanks Junior regularly travelled on the Cunarders, dancing the night away in the Queen Mary's Verandah Grill.

Greta Garbo wanted to be alone. She travelled incognito, disembarking from the Queen Mary disguised as a stewardess.

Film producer Sam Goldwyn travelled on the Queen Mary in the late 1930s. He always smoked a cigar even in the Turkish baths. Having no sense of direction he had to be led everywhere around the ship.

'The eighth wonder of the world' was how film star Cary Grant described his favourite liner. He regularly timed his trips across the Atlantic to fit in with the Queen Mary's sailing schedule. He met Betsy Drake, one of his five wives, when crossing on the ship in 1947.

Doris Hart, the Wimbledon tennis champion, learned how to play squash while travelling

with future champion Shirley Fry on the Queen Elizabeth.

Rita Hayworth the 'best dressed girl in Hollywood' liked to relax during trans-Atlantic crossings in sweater and slacks.

Legendary golfer Sam Snead travelled on the Queen Elizabeth in the early 1950s for the Ryder Cup. He hit golf balls round the squash courts, into the sea and even into the drain of the Turkish baths. He did not like to spend too much time there in case the perspiration destroyed his permanent sun tan.

When 'MGM's Golden Boy' Van Johnson travelled on the Queen Elizabeth in the early 50s, his wife refused to let him handle any money: she paid for everything on board.

For exercise on the Queen Elizabeth in the early 1950s film actor Burt Lancaster ran along the length of the boat deck and back on his hands. He once picked up his valet and left him swinging on an overhead rail outside the wardroom.

Kilted Scotsman Harry Lauder, the 'laird of the music hall', travelled on the Aquitania in the mid 1920s. He was a great hit with children, inviting them to sit in a ring around him on deck while he told stories and sang songs. The children joined in the chorus.

Actress and entertainer Gertrude Lawrence regularly broke the rules on the liners by exercising her dogs on the prom deck.

On a voyage on the Saxonia in the 1900s opera diva Nellie Melba's luggage was ruined when the hold was accidentally flooded: her famous opal dress had disintegrated, the opals lying in a heap in the bottom of the trunk. The chief officer was held responsible and lost his chance of promotion to captain.

Film star David Niven regularly kept passengers on the Queen Mary enthralled with stories of his colourful life. On one voyage his sons David (8) and Jamie (5) were so engrossed in playing in their father's cabin that the ship started to move with them still on board. Their father contacted the captain who ordered a tug to take them off, meaning a thirty foot descent from the ship's side.

Travelling on one of the Queens, cosmetics-queen Helena Rubinstein tossed her 20-carat diamond earrings out the porthole of her cabin. She forgot she had hidden them in the tissue box that she was discarding.

Actor Phil Silvers, the screen Sergeant Bilko, was the hairiest client that the Turkish Baths attendants on the Queens had ever massaged.

As Colonel Stewart, screen legend James Stewart returned from Second World War duties on the Queen Elizabeth. As the ship tied up at Pier 90, he commented to the ship's doctor: 'It's a long time since I had such a large lump in my throat. And there's strictly nothing you can do about that, doctor.'

Liners were part of the backdrop of film star Elizabeth Taylor's eight marriages. In 1950 she honeymooned with hotel chain heir Nicky Hilton on the Queen Elizabeth. Her new husband surprised passengers by playing cards in the smoking room until the small hours. She regularly travelled Cunard with her producer husband Mike Todd and partied all night with the actor Richard Burton whom she married twice.

In the mid 1930s Olympic swimmer and film star Johnny Weismuller used to swim up and down the Berengaria's pool making blood curdling Tarzan cries.

Above Bing, leaving the Queen Mary's darkroom with his latest prints.
Left Bing, about to embark, camera at the ready.

Bing Crosby was a regular on the Queen Mary. When he wanted to escape the crowds, he slipped into the photographic dark room, settled back in the same old chair, puffed away at his pipe and chatted to the photographers. He was soon roped in to help. He showed his gratitude by sending a large crate of beer to the dark room at the end of the voyage.

THE BUTCHER, THE BAKER
Unusual crew jobs

The makeup of a Cunarder's crew has changed dramatically over the last century and a half in line with technology and passenger expectations.

The Queen Mary's doctor Joseph Maguire contrasted the differences in the crew complement in the few years before and after the Second World War. 'There are radar operators now, officers expert in radio-telephony, assistant women pursers who deal with land and air travel inquiries and can take dictation from the fastest talking tycoon. The cinema operator has a full time job, usually handling six screenings each day. 'The butcher, the baker and the fancy cake maker have been joined by twenty two barmen, women and hairdressers, swimming instructors, liftmen, a kennel man, a Kosher cook, a gardener, Turkish Bath attendants, printers, photographers, a female telephonist and a physiotherapist.'

Some of the more unusual crew jobs have included:

The Baker Fresh bread was baked daily. The head baker was responsible for fancy work like cakes, the second and third baker would make the dough and the fourth baker would shape it into bread and rolls.

The Barber On late 19th century liners he supplemented his wages by selling postcards, toiletries and souvenirs.

The Black Squad Its members were the firemen, coal passers and trimmers who stoked coal and fed the boilers to keep the engines running.

The Bath Steward He looked after passengers' more basic needs from running baths to cleaning up. In the 1920s uniformed female bath attendants were introduced for lady passengers.

Opposite The Mauretania's Black Squad.

The Bellboy Aged 14-18 the bellboy was at the beck and call of passengers and crew, running messages all over the ship. One of their more unusual jobs on the Berengaria in the 1930s was to climb into the dome of the dining saloon and drop balloons on the guests on gala nights.

The Boots Steward He cleaned the shoes left overnight by passengers outside their cabin door. On deck he became a shoeshine boy.

The Crew Purser He assigned berths, inspected the crew's quarters and handled their financial affairs.

The Conductress As required by the Canadian government in the 1930s, she looked after female emigrants travelling on their own and unaccompanied children.

The Donkeyman In the early days of steam he looked after the donkey engine which supplied power to winches and pumps on deck when the main boilers were shut down.

Fruit Locker Man He was responsible for preparing all fruit and fruit juices as well as making up fruit baskets for presentation at dinner.

The Gardener As well as tending the plants daily he grew fresh vegetables and strawberries under glass, and cultivated mushrooms.

The Greaser Reporting to the donkeyman, he helped to oil the wheels and keep the engines running.

The Hospital Stewardess In the 1920s she was recruited essentially as a midwife because 'Quite a number of our steerage passengers have a habit of producing babies during the voyage.'

The Interpreter On late 19th century liners interpreters were often recruited from among third class passengers to assist emigrants who spoke no English.

The Kitchen Control Clerk By the 1930s the kitchens had become so complex that this post was created to write out menus, record the menu book, check stores and ensure that there was a smooth passage of dishes from kitchen to dining room.

The Lamp Trimmer Reporting to the Chief Officer, 'Lamps' were responsible for the upkeep of the decks. The name dates from the days of oil lighting when the lamp trimmer's job was to tend to the wicks.

The Master-at-Arms He was the ship's policeman, often accompanying Night Officers as they patrolled the decks or the captain on his tour of inspection. He kept a discreet eye on passengers especially at embarkation.

The Organist He was required to play everything from the latest Broadway hit to medleys of classical music and 'Eternal Father Strong to Save' on the organ in the Queen Mary's first class lounge.

The Printer Larger liners had a print shop to produce menus, the daily programme of events, the Ocean Times and onboard notices. The Queen Mary's print room produced 12,000 menus a day.

The Stenographer She was on call from the early 20th century to take shorthand from or type for businessmen on board.

The Steward's Boy He was at the bottom of the pecking order in the 1930s. 'I loaded bar stocks, removed dirty linen, scrubbed out toilets and cleaned cabins and stairs.'

The Tiger He was the Captain's personal steward. The name comes from the 18th century when masters of East Indiamen vied with each other to have the most gorgeously dressed servant.

Top (left to right) Carpenter on the Samaria II, Nursery Nurse on the Queen Elizabeth, Lift Attendant on the Britannic, Physiotherapist on the Queen Mary.
Middle (left to right) Engine Storekeeper on the Scythia II, Telephonist on the Caronia II, Second Baker on the Caronia II, Turkish Baths Attendant on the Queen Elizabeth.
Bottom (left to right) Bedroom Steward on the Queen Elizabeth, Shop Attendant on the Britannic.

The Turkish Baths Attendant He pounded, pummelled and massaged from early morning. He was also known as a good source of gossip about celebrities on board.

The Writer He was a member of the clerical team in the Purser's office who kept records of laundry, stores and similar transactions.

NOT ON THE MENU
Passenger food fads and fancies

In first class at least, it was Cunard policy to give passengers what they fancied even if not on the menu. A head waiter on the Queen Mary summed it up: 'The best food in the world without a doubt. Cunard didn't deny anything. If passengers wanted caviar for breakfast they got it.'

Testing 'Eat What you Fancy' to the limit in the 1950s, one US tycoon asked for rattlesnake steak. He was served eels on a silver platter by two stewards waving rattles. The tale was featured in a Cunard advertisement of the period under the headline - 'Will Your Requests Be As Outrageous as These?'

When Mr Kraft travelled on the Queens in the 1950s, Cunard featured his cheeses on the menu.

When honeymooning on the Mauretania II (1939), film star Lana Turner ordered raw minced beef with raw eggs beaten into it for breakfast, washed down by champagne.

Above Breakfast for troops on the Mauretania II (1939) was less exotic.

When travelling on the Queens, the actress and singer Frances Day brought her own hens to ensure that her eggs were fresh.

When travelling on the Queens, Elizabeth Taylor ordered special meals from the fish chef, not for herself but for her pet dogs.

Film star Victor Mature, 'the Screen Samson' had a gargantuan appetite. While crossing on the Queens he would demolish a 12 lb turkey at a sitting and order outsize steaks to be consumed in the Turkish baths. He always sent his compliments to the chef by autographing the menu with remarks like 'Cunard cooking is as great as sex - almost.' and 'To the only Chef, you're the greatest, and thank you for wrecking my career. Three stones a trip is impossible.'

One passenger on a crossing on the Queen Elizabeth in the 1950s was so fond of Watney's beer that he asked for a pint at the Chief Purser's cocktail party. 'No problem, Sir'.

One retired member of the QE2's crew recalled 'My favourite passengers were a couple from Texas. Lovely people but unfortunately all she lived on was caviar and vodka.'

Menus had to be adapted to the weather. In a storm those passengers who could face food at all demanded light plain dishes like bouillon or boiled vegetables rather than roast beef or sponge pudding.

In wartime choice was largely off the menu although many soldiers considered the food to be better than army rations. One soldier on his way to fight in Egypt during the First World War wrote home: 'Dinner 12.15: soup, roast or boiled meat, two vegetables and sometimes rice pudding. Tea 5.20: tea, butter rolls and stewed fruit, sausages or something of that sort.'

A GI on his way to Liverpool on the Caronia in 1918 fared less well. 'The wormy bread and half spoiled rabbit meat has furnished a fruitful topic of conversation. It was not many days out that Corporal 'Snake' Baublits proved that his stomach was not weak by putting his lunch the furthest overboard.'

Right
The Queen Mary's chef inspecting a batch of penguin eggs.

LINER LARDER

Food and drink stocked on the Cunarders

Impressive quantities of food and drink have always been carried on Cunarders.

Before refrigeration, supplies of fresh food only lasted a few days into the voyage. Cunard partly solved the problem by keeping a cow and hens on deck. Fresh vegetables were stored under the lifeboats.

'The quantities of wines, spirits, beer, etc put on board for consumption on the round voyage of the Etruria in 1886, comprise 1,100 bottles champagne, 850 bottles claret, 6,000 bottles ale, 2,500 bottles porter, 4,500 bottles mineral waters and 650 bottles various spirits.'

'As regards the consumption on board the whole Cunard fleet for one year, the figures seem almost fabulous: 4,656 sheep, 1,800 lambs, 2,474 oxen are consumed - an array of flocks and herds surpassing in extent the possessions of many a pastoral patriarch of ancient times - besides 24,075 fowls, 4,230 ducks, 2,200 turkeys, 2,200 geese, 53 tons of ham, 20 tons bacon, 15 tons cheese, and 832,603 eggs.'

Victualling Requirements and Stores of an Atlantic Liner, 1890

Left Stores being loaded on to the Aquitania in preparation for her maiden voyage (1914).

84 boxes of haddock, 12 barrels of red herring and 20 kegs of oysters were included in the regular fish order for the passengers and crew of the Lusitania.

The menu on the Queen Elizabeth's maiden voyage included Consomme Royale, Halibut Sauce Mousseline, Devilled Ham and Succotash, and Coupe Monte Carlo. This raised eyebrows in Britain, still suffering wartime rationing and food shortages, until Cunard pointed out that all ingredients except potatoes and fish had been purchased in the USA.

On a typical round crossing the Queen Elizabeth carried 40,000 lbs of flour, 2,100 lbs of peas and beans, 82,000 lbs of vegetables and 100,000 lbs of potatoes.

In the 1950s the Queens offered 16 different breakfast cereals.

Special occasions demanded extra supplies. During the 1954 Christmas season 13,000 passengers were at sea in seven Cunarders. On board were 65,000 lbs of poultry, 55,000 lbs of beef, 50,000 lbs of pork and veal, 300,000 eggs and 1500 large Christmas puddings.

In mid ocean a liner is entirely reliant on its supplies. In 1973, due to a slip up at the docks, the Cunard Adventurer ran out of tea in mid Atlantic. Afternoon tea was cancelled and the drink was strictly rationed and served at 5% strength until new supplies could be picked up in Barbados.

When turbine trouble left QE2 passengers in mid-ocean without water in 1974, Cunard offered unlimited champagne: some passengers even shaved in it.

The number of tea bags used each day on the QE2 would supply a family for a year.

Breakfasters on the QE2 snap crackle and pop their way through 770 packets of cereal a day.

The QE2 is the world's largest consumer of caviar. Nonetheless, pound for pound, the most expensive food item on board is saffron, 2.5 times the value of Beluga caviar.

The QE2's cellars carry 20,000 bottles of 203 different wines from 11 countries on four continents including 37 different champagne labels. Enough fruit juice is used in a year to fill up her swimming pools nearly eight times over.

LINER LINGO
The crew spoke their own language

'I joined the 'Ivy' (Ivernia II) late one afternoon in June. I had my first induction into the environment of gloryholes, working alleyways, black pans, tabnabs and a thousand other strange and wonderful words and expressions which will be engraved on my mind for the rest of my life.'

David Trotman, cook.

Aft end The stern or back end of the ship housing tourist class passengers

Barbareon Nickname for a female onboard hairdresser

Benders knees Put to hard use when scrubbing decks

Bibby alleyway A cul de sac

Black squad The firemen and trimmers who looked after the boilers

Bloods Passengers who could be bled dry for tips

B.R. Bedroom steward

Brass monkey Nickname for the Cunard house flag

On the bridge To be carpeted for a misdemeanour

Brightwork The metal fixtures that gleam through constant polishing by the crew

Broaching cargo Crew slang for having sex with a passenger

Bulkheads Referred to by passengers as walls

Bumboats Small boats that clustered round cruise liners selling fruit and groceries

Burma Road The main working alleyway that ran the length of the liner

Channel night The night before docking in Southampton

Chippy The ship's carpenter

Companionways Staircases

Cunard feet Big splay feet developed through years of carrying food on rolling liners

Cunard socks Bellboys who went barefoot in the tropics to keep cool were accused of wearing 'Cunard socks'

Cunard Yanks Crew who adopted American dress, style and taste in music in the 1950s

Deckheads Known by passengers as ceilings

Docking box Food kept aside by kitchen staff for the stewards

Ducer The second steward as opposed to the Boss, the first steward

Fiddleys or twiddlies The wooden surrounds attached to tables in rough weather

First tripper A crew member on their first voyage

Floating Fifth Avenue A large passenger liner

Fog chair The swivel chair on one of the bridge wings which was reserved exclusively for the captain's use in fog, in the days before radar

Galley Sports Day A thorough cleaning of the kitchen at the end of a crossing

Geraldo's navy Musicians who played in the liners' orchestras in the 1950s. Geraldo was the impresario who hired them

Glory hole The stewards' or engineers' quarters on a ship

The High Street Another name for the main crew alleyway

Holystones Soft sandstone blocks used to scrub the decks, part of the morning routine on early 20th century liners

Hot half crowns Small tips from third class passengers, so called because they held them for so long in their hand before parting with them

Idlers Crew like cooks and carpenters whose job exempted them from night watch duty

Logging Withholding pay for committing a fineable offence during the voyage

Middies Midshipmen

Mousses Bellboys

Nut crackers Money lenders whom some crew members had to visit regularly when in port

Peak Steward's accommodation situated in the liner's forepeak

Pig'n'Whistle The crew bar, also abbreviated to The Pig

Porthole thumb An injury sustained by passengers who tried to open their cabin porthole rather than summoning a steward with a key

Prince A member of the onboard print shop

Rosie Refuse bin

Scuttles Portholes

Scrambled egg The gold oak leaves on a captain's cap

Sea lawyers Crew whose critical remarks were designed to unsettle the smooth running of the ship

Ships' husbands Crew name for shipping line personnel and welfare staff

Side job A steward's routine tasks between meals

Slops Ready made clothing or shoes sold to the crew

Spud locker The vegetable preparation area of the kitchen

Strap up To clean silver

Sugi Hot soapy water

Tabnab A bun or pastry

Tick on To report for duty as a steward

Top side First class passenger accommodation

Vultures The marine equivalent of ambulance chasing lawyers who hung about the docks

Walkoff A stingy tipper

Wash-out duty Scrubbing the corridors and stairs, a less than popular duty with bellboys

Whites Uniform worn when sailing in the tropics

Wingers The name used by other crew to refer to waiters

Working alleyways Passages in the parts of the ship that the passengers never visited

'SAY, CAPTAIN'

Guests at the Captain's Table seized the opportunity to bombard him with questions. Here are a few of the commoner or more bizarre requests.

'The thing I want to know is who's driving the ship.'

'Is this the worst storm that you have ever experienced?'

'Does Cunard pay for your uniforms?'

'What time do you get up in the morning?'

'Do you know a reliable tailor in London?'

'If I post this letter today, when will it get to New York?'

'Captain, when does this place get there?'

'Have you ever been seasick?'

'Is this the same moon that I can see in Chicago?'

'How do you find your way across the Atlantic in the dark?'

'How do you get newspapers every morning?'

'Why are the deck lights left burning all day?'

To which one captain replied: *'In case we go through a tunnel.'*

Left Captain William Turner in full RNR rig, 1914.

'THANK YOU, SIR'

The fine art of tipping

When to tip and how much was a vexed question for inexperienced passengers and a matter of considerable interest to the crew. A good steward could earn more than the captain although, if caught soliciting tips, he faced dismissal.

'The jingling of coins plays too big a part in the life of the steward and he develops an uncanny gift for sizing folk up.'

Violet Jessop, stewardess, 1930s

'At the home port of a great liner you are quite likely to see a chief steward met at the quay by his chauffeur and limousine while the captain walks off towards an omnibus.'

Roydon Freeman, 'Sea Travel, the Serious Side and the Humorous Side', 1930

'Stewardesses were not at sea for their health or to admire this world so wide. They were there to get money, as much of it as could be skewered out of passengers at the end of a trip. People were 'all right' or 'no good' according to the tips they might give. Some passengers, decent ones, rewarded one in the privacy of their cabins, the ones who didn't must be waylaid, dogged and, if necessary, reminded.'

Maida Nixson, stewardess

The richest pickings were to be had from first class passengers bound for the Season in Europe. Deck stewards fared well in rough seas while bar stewards profited from the American habit of tipping after each drink as well as at the end of the voyage. Film stars were notoriously bad tippers, often regarding a signed publicity shot as sufficient reward for the honour of serving them. Royals were rumoured to be the worst tippers of all.

Large families were among the least popular passengers.

'You used to have a nanny or a governess with two or three children so at dinner you came down an hour earlier than you normally would do to serve them the meals and then you had to clear off and re-set again for the mother and father to come down and eat, and inevitably they were always the worst tippers.'

Waiter, Queen Mary

Tipping was also prevalent among the crew. A waiter would tip the cook to ensure that his clients were served the best steaks in the fastest possible time. He might also tip kitchen staff to put aside a helping from the first class menu for his own dinner.

'I used to clean portholes for the bedroom stewards when the Queen Mary docked in New York/Southampton and got paid $1 each porthole. My trick was to clean them in New York with Brasso then give them a coat of Vaseline so that when we got to Southampton I had only to remove the Vaseline!'

Waiter, Queen Mary, 1957

In 'The Frantic Atlantic' (1927), social commentator Basil Woon explained how a good steward earned his tips.

'A steward has to be an expert valet, he should be a good waiter, he must be unfailingly attentive and sympathetic, and, in cases of seasickness, he is frequently called upon to be a nurse. Their work is not finished when the ship reaches port - every cabin must be cleaned and aired and the laundry counted. A good steward is worthy of a good tip.'

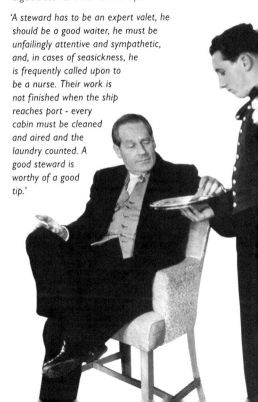

LINERS AND LANDMARKS

In order to impress the public with the sheer scale and might of its new liners, Cunard compared them to the wonders of the world.

The **Mauretania** was as long as London's Houses of Parliament.

The **Lusitania** was longer than the front of the world's largest cathedral, St Peter's in Rome.

It would take the slope of three of Egypt's largest pyramids to match the length of the **Aquitania**.

Babe Ruth's longest hit ball at the American League Baseball Stadium, New York could not outclass the **Berengaria** in length.

The **Queen Mary** was only 230 ft shorter than the Empire State Building, the world's highest building of the time. She was taller than the Niagara Falls and heavier than the entire Spanish Armada.

One of the promenade decks of the **Queen Elizabeth** was twice the length of the façade of Buckingham Palace.

Britannia, the very first Cunarder, could fit into the Grand Lounge of Queen Elizabeth 2.

Queen Mary 2 is the longest, tallest, widest and largest passenger vessel ever built. She is longer than the Eiffel Tower is tall and a foot higher than London's Tower Bridge.

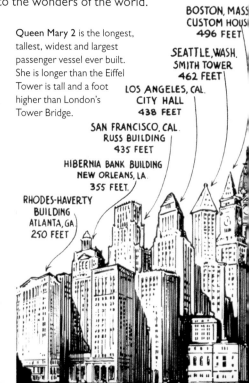

CHIC
BOARD
609

DETROIT, M
PENOBSCOT
557 FEE

PHILADELPHIA,
CITY HALL
548 FEET

BOSTON, MASS
CUSTOM HOUS
496 FEET

SEATTLE, WASH.
SMITH TOWER
462 FEET

LOS ANGELES, CAL.
CITY HALL
438 FEET

SAN FRANCISCO, CAL.
RUSS BUILDING
435 FEET

HIBERNIA BANK BUILDING
NEW ORLEANS, LA.
355 FEET.

RHODES-HAVERTY
BUILDING
ATLANTA, GA.
250 FEET

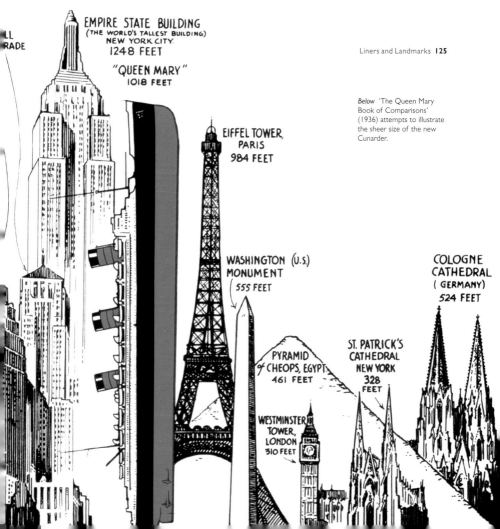

EMPIRE STATE BUILDING
(THE WORLD'S TALLEST BUILDING)
NEW YORK CITY.
1248 FEET

"QUEEN MARY"
1018 FEET

Below 'The Queen Mary
Book of Comparisons'
(1936) attempts to illustrate
the sheer size of the new
Cunarder.

EIFFEL TOWER,
PARIS
984 FEET

WASHINGTON (U.S.)
MONUMENT
555 FEET

COLOGNE
CATHEDRAL
(GERMANY)
524 FEET

PYRAMID
of CHEOPS, EGYPT
461 FEET

ST. PATRICK'S
CATHEDRAL
NEW YORK
328
FEET

WESTMINSTER
TOWER,
LONDON
310 FEET

LL
RADE

AT THE HELM
The captain's view of life onboard

Samuel Cunard knew exactly what he expected of his captains: 'Your ship is loaded, take her, speed is nothing; follow your own road, deliver her safe, bring her back safe ... safety is all that is required.'

Right from the start, however, captains were expected to entertain the passengers as well as command the vessel.

Charles Dickens, a passenger on the Britannia in 1842 wrote: 'The captain - who never goes to bed and is never out of humour - turns up his coat collar for the deck again; shakes hands all round and goes laughing out into the weather as merrily as to a birthday party.'

Captains had to live up to the copy of Cunard's publicity machine.

'The thoughtful onlooker cannot withhold a feeling of admiration for the man on the bridge, who has safely navigated the vessel over miles of turbulent ocean, and through all the perils, frequent enough of hurricanes, fogs and icebergs.'

'The Captain, lean as a Scottish loch, orders his guests like a flagged flotilla, deploying their movements with an expert touch and bringing them trimly alongside each other.'

Captains had to be good at meeting and greeting.

For three years after the Second World War, Captain Grattidge's only reading was 'Who's Who' and 'Who's Who in America'. Captain Robert Thelwell kept a list of the passengers that he had entertained on the Queens with comments for reference when drawing up future guest lists. Captain Robert Arnott of the QE2 once confided to his diary: '365 handshakes with incoming passengers in 34 minutes.'

Many captains did not take easily to retirement.

Commodore Geoffrey Marr who took the Queen Elizabeth on her final voyage in 1968 could not settle and signed on as second mate of a banana boat. Several captains settled down to write their memoirs. When Captain Edward

Treasure-Jones, last Captain of the Queen Mary, was asked why he had not followed this tradition, he replied 'Who'd read it?'

Occasionally captains were sorely tried.

Charles Judkins was one of Cunard's first captains, joining in 1840. He was famous for his temper. In mid Atlantic a lady passenger on the Scotia (1862) asked him how far the ship was from land. He gruffly replied: 'about a mile!' When she enquired: 'in which direction?' he pointed downward as he turned his back on her: 'In that direction, madam.'

One passenger lounging on the Berengaria's prom deck in the 1920s summoned Captain Irvine to remove her tray. There are two versions of his response. One is that he drew himself up to his full height and roared: 'And what the deuce do you suppose, ma'am, the Captain looks like.' The other is that he took the tray, threw it to the deck and replied: 'There, Madam, you can see what a very poor steward I am.'

Commodore Sir Ivan Thompson who captained the Queens in the 1950s was a fanatical Liverpool Football Club supporter. As soon as the results came in over the radio, they were sent to the bridge. If the news was bad, officers knew to keep out of his way for the rest of the day.

Right 'Every ship has three sides - port, starboard and social.' Commodore Arthur Rostron.

Captains were often given nicknames by the crew.

'Bowler Bill' Turner always wore a bowler hat when ashore.

'Logo' Lucas, a staff captain on the Franconia II during the Second World War liked to log or fine crew for misdemeanours.

Another captain of the Franconia II was **'One Engine' Woollatt**: the engines of his wartime ships kept breaking down.

'Tiger' Evans, master of the cargo vessel Vasconia (1948) liked to roar orders.

Captain **James 'Foggy' Barr** tended to reduce speed to a crawl at the first hint of a haze.

'Aughty Bill' Irvine, captain of the Berengaria in the 1920s, tended to look down his nose.

Even the captain could be embarrassed.

One captain on the Mauretania II (1939) decided to spruce up the ship when cruising in the West Indies by painting the funnels. By the time the liner reached New York, the temperature had dropped from the high nineties to -3F. It was so cold that the funnels had contracted a few inches and all the paintwork had fallen off in two foot square patches.

On entering New York Harbor it was traditional for liners to give a hoot. On the post-war maiden voyage of the Queen Elizabeth, the valve at the base of a funnel for the foghorn stuck and the foghorn sounded all the way from the Ambrose Light to Pier 90.

Captains were expected to achieve the impossible.

Only one request had Captain Grattidge stumped, when he looked after Winston Churchill on the Franconia II during the Yalta Conference in 1945. After visiting the battlefields, Churchill asked for de-lousing powder.

Opposite, top row, left to right
E.G. Lott (1840-1860), J. Pritchard (1840-1860), F. Jeffries (1880-1914), W.D. Cresser (1887-1922), D. Miller (1896-1924).

Opposite second row down, left to right
W. Williams (1877-1906), R. Warr (1880-1919), C. Morison (1885-1918), R.G. Malin (1889-1934), W. Prothero (1897-1932).

Opposite third row down, left to right
F.G. Brown (1900-1931), J. Johnston (1903-1923), H. McConkey (1904-1945), G.S. Horsburgh (1904-1937), G. Gibbons (1904-1932).

Opposite fourth row down, left to right
R.V. Peel (1900-1938), M. Doyle (1903-1931), W. Stafford (1904-1928), Sir R.B. Irving (1904-1932), R.D. Jones (1905-1942).

Opposite bottom row, left to right
W.A. Hawkes (1905-1945), G.R. Dolphin (1906-1940), W.C. Battle (1907-1945), P.A. Murchie (1905-1942), A.C. Greig (1906-1945).

FIRST CLASS... THIRD CLASS

Classes on the liners

Who you were and what you could afford was displayed on your luggage for all to see. On board until the 1960s your class of ticket also determined where you ate, slept and amused yourself.

'It cannot be urged too strongly that it is a gross breach of the etiquette of the sea life, and a shocking exhibition of bad manners and low inquisitiveness, for passengers to visit unasked the quarters of an inferior class.'

R. A. Fletcher: *Travelling Palaces: Luxury in Passenger Steamships*, 1913

The class system could be confusing. Over the last century and a half North Atlantic shipping lines have used over 30 names to describe different types of accommodation, ranging from First Class Upper Saloon to Steerage.

There were no classes on the first Cunarders. Passengers simply paid passage money. After the Collins Line entered the market in 1850, both Cunard and Collins divided accommodation into Chief Cabin and Second Cabin.

Cunard was slow to abandon Chief Cabin only replacing it by First Class or First Saloon in the 1880s. By 1900 4-6 berth Third Class cabins started to replace the dormitories of Steerage.

Although advance advertising for the Alaunia (1913) and the Andania (1913) offered Cabin (II) Passenger, this class was soon renamed One Class Cabin (Second Cabin).

When the USA closed its doors to emigration in the early 1920s, Cunard was the first North Atlantic shipping line to introduce a new class - Tourist Third - to attract young American holidaymakers 'doing Europe' on a budget. By 1950 Third Class had been renamed Tourist Class.

The Queen Mary wooed passengers by claiming that her Third Class accommodation was more luxurious than Cabin Class on other liners. The price of a first class ticket in 1936 could keep a family with three children in food for over a year.

In the 1930s Cunard renamed First Class Cabin Class but in 1950 announced 'Once again top class quite properly becomes FIRST CLASS as it always has been in quality.'

The QE2 was Cunard's first classless ship, the standard of accommodation simply linked to the price of the ticket.

25 BROADWAY
Cunard's American headquarters

Around 1850 Cunard opened a New York Office in Bowling Green, the shipping district close to the Piers which became known as 'Steamship Row'. When the site was wanted for the new US Custom House around 1900, Cunard moved several times within the district before deciding to build a North American headquarters in keeping with its 'grand hotels at sea'.

Designed by Benjamin Wistar Morris, the 22 storey skyscraper took four years from concept to completion. One engineering challenge was erecting the building over the curving subway tunnel that bisected the site. The exterior with its frontage of Indiana limestone was relatively plain to blend in with the canyon-like streets of Lower Manhattan. Marine-inspired sculptures enlivened the sober facades, the keystones symbolising the Four Winds and the entrances crowned with the head of Neptune.

Right The Great Hall (1921).
Opposite top left Menu, with the Cunard Building on the left, (1955).
Opposite top right The central dome of the Great Hall, (1921).

Travellers passing through the portals were left in no doubt that they were dealing with the world's most prestigious shipping line. The 185 ft long Great Hall which served as the ticket office was modelled on Classical Roman baths and villas whose 'influence pervades the whole, subtle and intangible, like the smell of incense in an ancient shrine.' In the same 1930s brochure Cunard described how 'the eye and mind are at once impressed with a sense of space and dignity unusual in a room designed to transact business.' The ultimate marvel was the domed ceiling, decorated with a myriad of ships and sea creatures.

Cunard occupied the first four floors of the building and the top floor with its stunning views over Manhattan, reached by 33 high speed elevators. It leased the rest of the office space to other shipping lines, banks and corporate headquarters. In 1968 Cunard moved to its present office at 555 Fifth Avenue while the Great Hall of 25 Broadway is now a branch of the US Postal Service.

'SAY, WHEN DOES THE BAR OPEN?'
Cunard during Prohibition

Ever since 1840 passengers and crew have enjoyed a drink on board. On the Britannia the wine and spirits bar opened at 6am: in those days passengers were roused at five to allow staterooms to be swept out. The crew also enjoyed a tipple, causing Charles Dickens to complain in 1842: 'The ship's cook, secretly swigging damaged whiskey, has been found drunk; and has been played upon by the fire-engine until quite sober.'

Alcohol or the lack of it became a serious issue during Prohibition (1920-1933), some Americans travelling on British registered liners simply in order to get a drink. Weekend 'booze cruises' were popular. As the Mauretania sailed past the Statue of Liberty, one desperate passenger greeted an officer: 'Say, that statue's gone. The bars will be open, won't they?'

'In the early days of Prohibition, the passengers would hang around the bars until the ship passed the three mile limit and as soon as they opened up, a roaring trade would be done. Everyone seemed to think that any minute the ship might go dry too.'

Charles Spedding, purser on the Carmania.

Pantry stewards had to keep later hours and the larger ones doubled up as bouncers. On eastbound trips on the Aquitania the ship's doctor treated cases of the DTs and a few passengers were stretchered off at Southampton. On some westbound crossings the sale of spirits was banned to third class passengers for fear of emigrants making the most of their last chance to get drunk.

Occasional excesses continued even after the end of Prohibition. When the American Liquor Dealers hired the Mauretania II for a sales executives' incentive cruise during the 1950s, they brought their own booze by the barrel load. Captain Bob Arnott later recalled:

LIST OF PRICES

FOR

WINES, SPIRITS, AND OTHER LIQUORS.

WINES.

		Per Quart. s. d.	Per Pint. s. d.
CHAMPAGNE,	**WACHTER'S** extra Cuvée, as selected for Her Majesty, the Prince of Wales, and other members of the Royal Family.		
	HEIDSIECK & CO., Dry Monopole.		
	ROEDERER		
	G. H. MUMM & CO., Carte Blanche, and Extra Dry.		
	RUINART PÈRE ET FILS, Dry Pale Cremant.	7 6	4 0
	PERRIER-JOUËT & CO., Pale Dry Creaming.		
	KRUG & CO., Carte Blanche. ...		
	BOLLINGER, Dry Extra Quality. ...		
CLARET, FIRST QUALITY		6 0	3 6
Do. SECOND QUALITY		3 6	2 0
HOCK		5 0	3 0
SPARKLING HOCK		5 0	3 0
Do. MOSELLE		5 0	3 0
Do. BURGUNDY		6 0	—
PORT		4 0	—
SHERRY		4 0	—
MADERIA		7 6	—
CHARTREUSE (LIQUEUR)		—	5 0
LIQUEUR GINGER BRANDY (BRETT'S "NEGRO-HEAD")		—	—

SPIRITS.

		Per Pint. s. d.	Per Glass. s. d.
BRANDY	... ...	3 0	0 6
WHISKY (DUBLIN)	... ...	2 6	0 6
(The famous brands of John Jameson & Son, Wm. Jameson & Co., Sir John Power & Son, and George Roe & Co.)			
WHISKY (SCOTCH)	... ...	2 6	0 6
HOLLANDS	... ...	4 0	0 6
OLD TOM	... ...	3 0	0 6

Ale, 6d. Porter, 6d. Soda Water, 6d. Ginger Ale, 6d. Lemonade, 6d. English Seltzer, 6d. German Seltzer, 1s. Congress Water, 1s. Kali Potass, 6d. Sarsaparilla, 6d.

ALL, EXCEPT WINES, TO BE PAID FOR ON DELIVERY.

The Steward is directed to Present and Collect the Wine Bills against Passengers on the day previous to the Ship's Arrival.

43

'I don't think I have never seen so much liquor sloshing around one ship. So many parties were going on that no-one, it seemed, ever finished a drink. So much wasted liquor was poured down the drains by stewards that one of them swore to me that he had heard a following school of dolphins hiccupping all over the Caribbean.'

Help for hangovers was at hand. In the 1950s bedroom stewards on the Queens would discreetly recommend a trip to the Turkish baths. There the attendants administered three steam baths, a cold shower and a bowl of French onion soup.

Left 1878 price list.

SKIPPERS ALL
Cunard in verse

From amateurs to Poet Laureates, people have been moved to express their feelings for the liners in verse.

'How timid and slow, but a few years ago,
The world hobbled on in its motion
Old Europe seem'd far as the fix'd Northern Star
On the boundless expanse of the ocean
But though it were hard – at the word of Cunard
Britannia herself is a rover
Old England awhile, that fast anchor'd isle
By steam is now here – half seas over.'

Song to celebrate the arrival of the Britannia in Boston, 1840

'The boat-express is waiting your command!
You will find the Mauretania at the quay,
Till her captain turns the lever 'neath his hand,
And the monstrous nine-decked city goes to sea.'

Rudyard Kipling,
'The Secret of the Machines'

'In uniform a-standing,
observe the chest expanding.
How the linen is outstretched,
personality does the rest.
The value of knowing when to smile or frown,
Has helped many a one to fame and renown.
Even the knowledge of an angle to a fine degree,
That the cap fits the uniform best at sea.'

John Hampton Chadwick, ' Skippers All: Breezy Sketches Set in Rhyme of Prominent Cunard Skippers Whom I have Met', 1915

'With cash book and ruler, pencil and pen,
He enters the wages paid to the men.
And should some rude sailorman grumble and curse,
He gently admonishes him in blank verse.'

Anon, writing about John Hampton Chadwick,
Cunard Magazine, 1921

Soliloquies .
~Grave & Gay~
of . . .
Ye Olde . .
Cunard Office .

By

John Hampton Chadwick

Xmas 1916.

Soliloquies
Grave and Gay
of
Ye Olde Cunard Office.

Like an old hulk, now left here stranded,
With auction bills and signs I'm branded,
I've served my turn, and now they're left me -
Shorn of my emblems have bereft me.
My flag-staff towers as a mast,
Where flew the old flag in the past,
Proudly I wore it on sailing day
Now 'cept at night, floats it away.

O'er seventy years, since all, or either
Sam'l Cunard, Burns and MacIver
Conceived the "Vital North American".
Aye! what things have happen'd in that span!
The line has grown to such dimensions,
Beyond all dreams in their intentions,
[...] that nursed them till they grew so great,
As now nursed in a Bankers' Estate.

Great mortals, sure, have pass'd my portals -
Lords, Ladies and all sorts of mortals.
For shipping, life rides, time and [...]
As cheerful as the wind that blows
[...] eighteen sixty they changed my style -
Tho' known as the Cunard all the while -
Run by Managing Agents, then
With staff, composed chiefly, of Gentlemen.

(2)

Soon after, in the high speed fevers,
Came dispute 'twixt Burns and MacIvers,
John Burns, erstwhile The Lord Inverclyde,
Meant the flag on top, what'er betide.
On policy question they fell out -
A critical time, without a doubt -
To shape the course - maintain the prestige,
Was surely a great privilege.

See, now, how famous the Line has grown -
Good men, at helm, has she always known,
Who've steered her safe through all storm and stress.
Her course was always one of progress,
Wise counsel at the Board are given,
Where all have for one purpose striven
And proud is Britannia, of the Line
Now dominated by the Combine.

What evolution have I not seen
From the Paddle-Boat to big Turbine?
Some day it may not be thought insane
To cross the Ocean by Aeroplane!
And from their own lofty roof garden near by
Crowds wave farewells as air-ships fly!
But then I'll be sizing up vast sums,
In Bankers' Ledgers - when that day comes.

To Marion Shaw Chadwick
with the best wishes
of her uncle, the Author
24 Feb 1916

SKIPPERS ALL

BREEZY SKETCHES, SET IN RHYME,

OF PROMINENT

CUNARD SKIPPERS

WHOM I HAVE MET.

BY

J. H. C.

DECEMBER, 1915.

Right J.H.C. was John
Hampton Chadwick, an
accountant in Cunard's head
office who privately published
several volumes of verse
about the shipping line.

' ... this, a rampart of a ship,
Long as a street and lofty as a tower,
Ready to glide in thunder from the slip
And shear the sea with majesty of power.

I long to see you leaping to the urge
Of the great engines, rolling as you go,
Parting the seas in sunder in a surge,
Shredding a trackway like a mile of snow.'

John Masefield, 'No 534' written to mark the launch of the
Queen Mary, 1934

'There were ships of oak in the days of old
There are ships of steel today
And the song is the same from the men who build
'God speed her on her way.'
A Toast to the Queen Mary
Long may she sail the sea
Here's to the name she bears
Here's to the course she steers.'

Ina George, spectator at the launch of the
Queen Mary

'Somewhere at sea,
a liner is somewhere at sea
Bringing to me a traveller
Who will fill my life anew
She's out on the sea
Sailing to me, sailing to me.'

Song sung by **Frances Day** with the backing
of the Henry Hall Orchestra during the
Queen Mary's maiden voyage, 1936

'When your life seems to difficult to rise above
Sail away, sail away
When your heart feels as dreary as a worn-out glove
Sail away, sail away
But when soon or late
You recognise your fate
That will be your great, great day
On the wings of the morning with your own true love
Sail away, sail away, sail away.'

Noel Coward, 'Sail Away'

'Early morning fast needs breakin
Eggs n ham n griddle cakes
Fried tomatoes crispy bacon
Choc'late malted milky shakes
Now eleven coffee calling
Cookies brown n donuts round
Time for lunch and one meatball in
Salad French and pepper ground.'

Cunard waiter and rock star **Tommy Steele**,
'Higher Waffle or How I had my first trip as a
blood on the Cunard'

'With her record for war or peace unsurpassed,
Meeting her duty to the last,
When she retires from the Atlantic
at the end of the year,
She'll still be the Queen with a new career.'

Poem iced on cake celebrating the final
voyage of the Queen Elizabeth, 1968

WRITER ON BOARD
Authors' reflections on Cunarders

Authors crossed the Atlantic for lecture tours, book signings, negotiations with Hollywood or simply to relax. This is how a few of them described their crossing.

'That this state-room had been specially engaged for 'Charles Dickens, Esquire, and Lady' was rendered sufficiently clear even to my scared intellect by a very small manuscript, announcing the fact, which was pinned on a very flat quilt, covering a very thin mattress, spread like a surgical plaster on a most inaccessible shelf.'

Charles Dickens, passenger on the Britannia, 1842

'And so through storm and darkness, through fog and midnight, the ship had pursued her steady way over the pathless ocean and roaring seas, so surely that the officers who sailed her knew her place within a minute or two, and guided us with a wonderful providence safe on our way.'

William Makepeace Thackeray, passenger on the Canada, 1852

'I don't like some of these vessels. Some of them keep a man hungry all the time unless he has a good appetite for boiled rice. I know some steamers where they have the same bill of fare they used to have when the company ran sailing packets: beans on Tuesday and Friday, stewed prunes on Thursday, and boiled rice on Wednesday; all very healthy, but very bad. But we are fed like princes aboard here, and have made a comfortable voyage.'

Mark Twain of his crossing on the Gallia, 1879

'The world looked cheerful enough until, on the third day, the world - as far as concerned the young man - ran into a heavy storm. He learned then a lesson that stood by him better than any university teaching ever did - the meaning of a November gale on the mid-Atlantic which, for mere physical misery, passed endurance.'

Henry Adams, travelling on the Persia, 1858

'Once a week comes a Cunard steamer, with its red funnel pipe whitened by the salt spray; and, firing off cannon to announce her arrival, she moors to a large iron buoy in the middle of the river, and a few hundred yards from the stone

Above On the deck of the Gallia.

pier of our ferry. Immediately comes puffing towards her a little mail-steamer, to take away her mail-bags and such of the passengers as choose to land; and for several hours afterwards the Cunard lies with the smoke and steam coming out of her, as if she were smoking her pipe after her toilsome passage across the Atlantic.'

Nathaniel Hawthorne writing of his time as US Consul in Liverpool, 1853-7

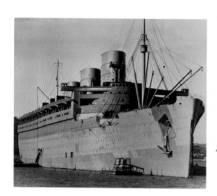

'I remember her dazzling speed and the graceful way she would lean over into the zigzags to frustrate the undersea wolf packs.'

Paul Gallico writing about the Queen Mary during the Second World War

'She was slow, but she was spacious and comfortable and there was a kind of motherly decency in her long, nursing rock and her rustling old fashioned gait. It was as if she wished not to present herself in port with the splashed eagerness of a young creature.'

Henry James, passenger on the Servia, 1883

'I liked the idea of dressing for dinner and seeing everything quite stately and formal. The little be-buttoned call-boys in their tight-fitting blue suits amused me. And the bugler who bugled for dinner! That was a most musical sound he made, trilling the various quarters gaily, as much as to say: 'This is a very joyous event, ladies and gentlemen; we are all happy; come, it is a delightful feast.'

Theodore Dreiser, passenger on the Mauretania

'Heavy seas, mountainous meals, a movie each afternoon, ten hours of sleep each night, an ever-open bar – all these have proved very beneficial. We are both relishing these days of suspended animation. Little walks on the icy deck, bowls of broth at 11am, tea and light music after the movie, visits to the library punctuate the steady rhythm of creaking timbers, throbbing floors and rushing waters.'

Rupert Hart-Davis travelling on the Queen Mary, 1961

STOCKING A LINER
Crockery and linen on board

Checking and replacing the stores on a liner was a mammoth task.

'Crockery is broken very extensively, being at the rate of 900 plates, 280 cups, 438 saucers, 1,213 tumblers, 200 wine-glasses, 27 decanters, and 63 water-bottles in a single voyage.'

Victualling Requirements and Stores of an Atlantic Liner, 1890.

There was regular wear and tear. On the Queens in the 1950s over half a million pieces of china, glass and cutlery were used every day to serve 10,000 meals. Rough seas could play havoc with stores. In the 1950s, before the Queen Mary was fitted with stabilisers, up to 25,000 pieces of crockery could be broken in a year.

Opposite The Queen Mary Book of Comparisons (1936) illustrates the scale of housekeeping.

Liners had to be kept spick and span at sea. In 1935 the stores departments of the Aquitania purchased:

636 tins of bath powder
480 gallons of white paint
972 tins of metal polish
225 gallons of black paint
409 kegs of soft soap
230 gallons of deck varnish
1400 gallons of liquid soap
225 gallons of detergent
492 scrubbing brushes
294 carpet brooms
180 brooms

Once a year, each Cunarder tied up for a serious spring cleaning. The overhaul of an average liner in the 1950s involved 15,000 gallons of paint, 100 broom handles, 1000 electric lamps, 1000 tons of sand to 'scrub the decks to pristine whiteness' and 500 gallons of lubricating oil.

LINEN SUPPLIES
210,000 TOWELS
30,000 SHEETS
31,000 PILLOW CASES
AND THOUSANDS of
OTHER PIECES

21,000
TABLE CLOTHS

92,000
NAPKINS

OVER
HALF A MILLION
PIECES of CHINA,
GLASS-WARE AND
TABLE SILVER ARE IN USE

OVER 40,000 MEALS, PREPARED IN THE
MODERN ELECTRIC RANGES AND OVENS,
ARE SERVED DURING A SINGLE TRIP

Stocking also depended on who was travelling. Even the allocation of salt and pepper depended on class, first class passengers having one set between two people while second and third class had to make do with one set among three.

Salt and pepper sets were also popular with souvenir hunters. Guests at the party to celebrate the end of the QE2's maiden voyage wrapped hundreds of them in linen napkins and took them home as keepsakes. Next day replacement sets had hastily to be purchased from Woolworths.

The linen stores were prodigious. The Queens each had 30,000 bed sheets, 210,000 towels, 31,000 pillowcases and 21,000 table cloths while in 1969 the QE2 was stocked with 8,600 blankets, 23,000 sheets, 26,200 pillow cases, 26,000 bath towels, 31,000 hand towels, 1500 deck rugs and 14,000 glass towels.

In a typical year the QE2 uses over 2 million doilies, over a million napkins, 125 miles of aluminium foil and enough cling film to go round the vessel nearly 731 times. When cruising she takes on a quarter of a million toilet rolls and 10,000 spare light bulbs.

TROOPING
Statistics of war

As part of the contract with Cunard, the British Government could call up the Line's ships for war service.

During the Crimean War (1854-1856) 11 Cunarders carried over 100,000 troops and 7500 horses slung in hammocks on the decks.

In the Second Boer War (1899-1902) eight Cunarders travelled 404,713 miles with a total of 75,000 troops, refugees and prisoners on board.

During the First World War (1914-1918) Cunard vessels steamed 3,313,576 miles and carried 1,000,000 troops. Half of the total North American contingent crossed on Cunarders. The shipping line managed 400 vessels on behalf of the UK Government.

In the Second World War (1939-1945) Cunard carried 9,223,181 tons of cargo and 2,223,040 troops. Nearly half travelled on the Queens and the Aquitania. Only nine of the 18 passenger vessels called up for service survived the War.

The Queen Elizabeth made 64 crossings, the Queen Mary 60 and the Aquitania 50 during the Second World War. On most Atlantic runs the Queens transported the equivalent of a US Army division.

Right Troops gather on the deck of the Queen Mary.
Above Queen Elizabeth heading out of Cape Town during WW2.

On 25th-30th July, 1943 the Queen Mary carried the greatest number of people ever to board a ship - 15,740 troops and 943 crew.

THE THIRD GRACE

Cunard's Liverpool headquarters

From 1917 until 1967 Cunard had its headquarters on Liverpool's Pier Head, looking out over the estuary of the Mersey. Modelled on the Farnese Palace in Rome, the building was erected on the site of the 18th century George's Dock whose walls still form part of the foundations.

Statistics give a feel for the scale of construction. The building used 57,755 tons of material including 150,000 cu ft of Portland stone, 50,000 cu ft of granite and 700,000 cu ft of concrete. Laid end to end the 2000 tons of steel bars, used to reinforce the concrete, stretched 1000 miles. The eleven floors could pack in a quarter of a million people.

The Cunard Empire was ruled from the fifth floor with its board room, naval architects' department, directors' dining room and 'accommodation for lady stenographers'. Over a thousand employees worked in the building from the hydrographer who mapped the world's tides from his roof-top eyrie to the experimental chef who tested new dishes like frog's legs on the staff.

On the ground floor was the ticket hall and lounge for first class passengers. 'The intending passenger visiting the Cunard Building must carry away a mental picture in which massive grandeur, chaste refinement, and a general pervading air of comfort have been artistically blended.' Second and third class passengers were dealt with in the basements along with the stores, safes and luggage.

Emigrants often had to face the ordeal of a medical examination and forms to complete before embarking. Cunard was anxious to reassure them that they will experience in the efforts made to enhance their comfort, some little foretaste of that unremitting care and attention which has won for Cunard ships a unique reputation with this class of ocean traveller.'

Cunard headquarters and the buildings on either side, became known as the Three Graces because of their magnificent architecture and waterfront setting. Today they are protected as a UNESCO World Heritage site.

Left An artists impression of the Cunard building
Below, from left The Three Graces, an eagle perches in the main hall and exploring the luggage hall, which today remains as it was left in the 1960s.

THE CUNARD YANKS

Liverpool seafarers in New York

The Cunard Yanks were a group of young stewards, pantrymen and waiters whose style took their home port of Liverpool by storm in the early 1950s. New York shops were packed with novelties and goods that were like gold dust in grey, war-battered Britain. The city's clubs and radio stations were buzzing with new sounds, from early R'n'B to Cool Jazz.

While on leave in New York, the Cunard Yanks filled their bags with presents for family and girlfriends - plastic dolls, nylons, tinned food, fridges, Frank Sinatra hats, nappy pins, movie cameras, blow up toys, and even a juke box for a local Liverpool pub.

The Cunard Yanks dressed differently, wore aftershave and adopted American hair styles. Their midnight blue mohair suits, slip-on shoes and button-down or tab-collar shirts made them stand out in the Liverpool dancehalls where de-mob suits and army coats were the norm.

'I used to have a pink suit with elegant thin trousers: no-one had ever seen the like.'

They also brought back the latest records from black artistes, many of whom had never been heard in the UK. These records influenced the development of the distinctive Liverpool Sound which in turn led to the Beatles and the Mersey Beat. George Harrison is supposed to have purchased his first 'real American guitar', a 1957 Duo Jet Gretsch, through a Cunard Yank.

The Cunard Yanks still remember the electric effect they had on their home city.

Main image The sign of Pier 90 that used to greet arrivals into New York

'Everyone knew you were a seaman: they'd know where you'd been by your tie and your suits. We bought them in Sachs, in New York.'

A CRIME THAT STAGGERED HUMANITY

The loss of the Lusitania

Although the Lusitania (1907) was a floating Grand Hotel and Blue Riband holder, she was designed for conversion into an armed cruiser in the event of war. When war was declared in 1914, however, she continued to cross as a passenger liner.

On 22nd April, 1915, on the same page as the announcement of the Lusitania's sailing, the New York Times carried a warning from the German Embassy in Washington that passengers on British or allied ships travelled at their own risk. On the eve of the liner's departure nine days later, American multi-millionaire Alfred G. Vanderbilt received an anonymous telegram: 'Have it on definite authority the Lusitania is to be torpedoed. You had better cancel passage immediately. - Morte' Vanderbilt chose to ignore Morte's death threat.

Flying the American flag for protection, the Lusitania left for Liverpool with 1959 passengers and crew on board. At 2.10pm on 7th May, as she reached the busy sea lanes off the Irish coast, the commander of U-boat U-20 spotted the four funnels of a big kill. Eighteen minutes later after two devastating explosions, the Lusitania sank with the loss of 1201 men, women and children.

Shortly after the disaster a German commercial artist designed a medallion satirising what he saw as British irresponsibility in allowing the Lusitania to sail in U-boat infested waters. On one side three images of a sinking, heavily armed ship were titled 'No Contraband Goods': the other side depicted a skeleton handing out tickets at a Cunard Line office with one man in the queue reading a newspaper. Its headline satirised the British approach - 'Geschäft über alles' (Business above all).

One of the first batch of medallions, accidentally but incorrectly dated 'May 5', fell into British hands, fuelling rumours that the attack on the Lusitania had been planned in advance. British naval intelligence seized the propaganda opportunity to sell around 300,000 replicas to the public with the proceeds going to charity.

The propaganda kept alive the memory of the Lusitania in the minds of a public numbed by news from the trenches. The disaster also helped to bring America into the War.

Above and opposite Front and reverse of the Lusitania medal.

LUSITANIA ROAD

LEADING TO MAURETANIA ROAD

SHIP STREET
Liverpool streets named after the liners

Even on shore leave some Liverpool seafarers could not escape from the liners. Several streets in Cunard's home port were named after the ships that tied up in Gladstone Dock or berthed at the Pier Head. Many captains and officers chose to live in the villas and terraces overlooking the Mersey estuary where they could hear the sea as they lay in bed. The 'black squad' and deck hands were more likely to stay in the steep streets of red brick 'two up, two down' terraces running off the Scotland Road.

FELLOW PASSENGERS

Onboard photographers captured the rich, the famous and ordinary passengers having fun

'At sea you are not anonymous. The time and pleasure are yours. indeed an Atlantic crossing, either way - far more than a means of just getting there - can be a social event, a luxurious party, a long week-end with distinguished company.'

Author **Laurie Lee** first class passenger on the Queen Mary 1960.

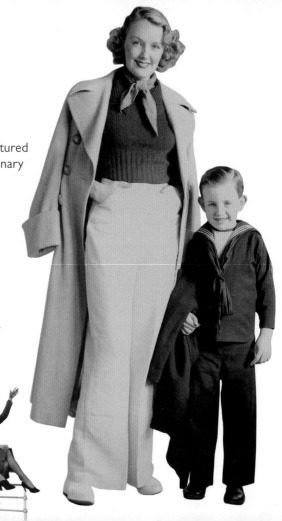

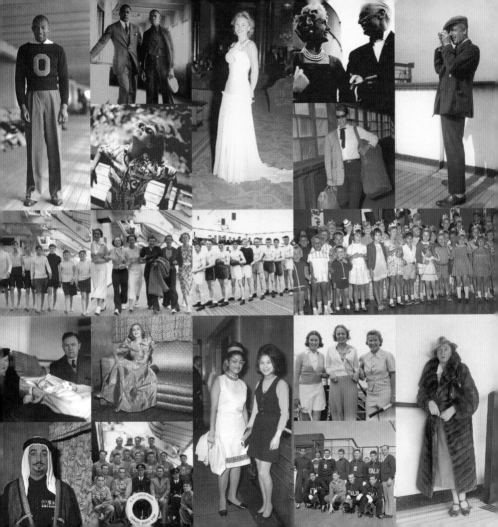

CUNARDIA

A *AMEN* telegraph operators' shorthand for 'Arrived, all well stormy passage'
B *BUGLE* sounded to summon passengers to dinner
C *CENTRAL 9201* the telephone number of Cunard's Liverpool HQ in the 1950s
D *DINNER JACKET* without which 'you will have no dances and no Great Moments' (1927)
E *ELLIS ISLAND* where immigrants were inspected before landing in New York
F *FINNISH* one of the 18 languages covered in the Queen Mary's library
G *GANGPLANK WILLIES* New York's pier head newspaper reporters
H *HOLYSTONE* used to scrub the liners' decks
I *ICE SCULPTURE* the art of the confectionery cook for gala dinners
J *JEROBOAM* equivalent to four bottles of champagne, served at the Captain's Table
K *KAYSER SILK* the recommended material for ladies underwear to avoid seasickness
L *LIVERPOOL FLYER* the non-stop boat train from London Euston
M *MAIL SACKS* which prisoners made up specially for Samuel Cunard
N *NAPKIN* a million of which are used on the QE2 a year
O *OCEAN PICTURES* whose onboard photographers snapped the passengers
P *PIER 90* the main berth for the Queens in New York
Q *QUARTET* in third class, sextet in second and octet in first, playing during afternoon tea
R *REGENT STREET* the name of the Queen Mary's shopping arcade
S *STOCK EXCHANGE* operated on board the Berengaria during the Great Crash
T *TIGER* the personal servant to the captain
U *UMBRELLA* the cone shaped shield at the top of the smoke stack
V *VIBRO FACE MASSAGE* available from the Queens' barbers for 3/6d
W *'WANTED ON VOYAGE'* indicating that luggage was to be sent to the owner's cabin
X *XMAS PIES* 50,000 of which were baked for the festive season at sea in 1951
Y *YEW* one of the 56 varieties used on the Queen Mary 'the ship of beautiful woods'
Z *ZIG-ZAG* the manoeuvre performed by wartime Cunarders to avoid U-boats